C000311618

On the
Same Side

ISBN: 1-4129-1079-X

 Published by Lucky Duck
Paul Chapman Publishing
A SAGE Publications Company
1 Oliver's Yard
55 City Road
London EC1Y 1SP

SAGE Publications, Inc.
2455 Teller Road
Thousand Oaks, California 91320

SAGE Publications India Pvt Ltd
B-42, Panchsheel Enclave
Post Box 4109
New Delhi 110 017

www.luckyduck.co.uk

Commissioning Editor: George Robinson
Editorial Team: Mel Maines, Sarah Lynch, Wendy Ogden
Translator: Louis Ingouville
Designer: Helen Weller

© Francisco Ingouville 2005

All rights reserved. No part of this publication may be reproduced, stored in a retrieval system, or transmitted in any form, or by any means, electronic, mechanical, photocopying, recording or otherwise, without the prior, written permission of the publisher.

The right of the Author to be identified as Author of this work has been asserted by him/ her in accordance with the Copyright, Design and Patents Act, 1988.

Printed in Great Britain by The Cromwell Press Ltd, Trowbridge, Wiltshire.

On the Same Side

133 Stories to Help Resolve Conflict

Francisco Ingouville

Translated by Luis Ingouville

P·C·P
Paul Chapman
Publishing

Lucky Duck is more than a publishing house and training agency. George Robinson and Barbara Maines founded the company in the 1980s when they worked together as a head and as a psychologist, developing innovative strategies to support challenging students.

They have an international reputation for their work on bullying, self-esteem, emotional literacy and many other subjects of interest to the world of education.

George and Barbara have set up a regular news-spot on the website at http://www.luckyduck.co.uk/newsAndEvents/viewNewsItems and information about their training programmes can be found at www.insetdays.com

More details about Lucky Duck can be found at http://www.luckyduck.co.uk

Visit the website for all our latest publications in our specialist topics

- Emotional Literacy
- Self-esteem
- Bullying
- Positive Behaviour Management
- Circle Time
- Anger Management
- Asperger's Syndrome
- Eating Disorders

To reach the author:

Francisco Ingouville

Ingouville & Nelson Training and Consultancy

francisco@ingouvillenelson.com.ar

www.ingouvillenelson.com.ar

Acknowledgements

This book is a very heartfelt acknowledgement to the people who told me great stories. In passing them on, I endorse not only those stories but also a vocation for spreading ideas, for sharing emotions, for thinking, for laughing, and for changing… together.

It must be practically impossible to know how many stories are passed on orally within a community every day. However, one can intuitively tell that the pulsation of stories through a social network carries out an important function.

A story can transmit ideas we have yet to clarify in our minds. It can reach remote corners of our mind where we find theory somewhat rigid or dull to absorb. It has visual images which our mind can retrieve sooner, whenever necessary. And it is capable of taming that combative and territorial animal we carry deep in our brain cortex. Stories constituted an initial cultural link for pre-historic communities gathered around the fire, as well as for most of us as children. When at times I use a story to illustrate a point during a course for government officials or business people, I enjoy watching the audience relax snugly in their seats, as both the child and the primitive creature every decision-maker carries inside, celebrates from within. I've been there, at the listening end, when I first came across these stories, and I know just what it feels like.

Until now, I used to think acknowledgements in books were mere formalism. Not any more. Throughout the years I worked on this book, I felt deeply indebted for priceless help received on countless opportunities. It is true that without some of this help I simply could not have finished the job. Had Carmen and our children not backed up my graduate course project at Harvard University… had Luis and the Ingouville Publicidad team not supported me from Buenos Aires… had my classmate Horacio Falcão not encouraged and helped me getting the idea off the ground… if the professors, mediators, negotiators and fellow-students I interviewed had not so generously shared their knowledge, stories and anecdotes… this book could not have been written.

It is so obvious that this book is a product of the co-operation of many people (including those who took the opposing side in my conflicts) and they make up such a long list, that I will only mention a few.

Peter Tarak, who I had great pleasure working with at FARN, and thanks to whom I took my first mediation courses. Yolanda Kakabadse, who delivered one of these courses, and opened up a thousand doors for me since. Gabriel Griffa, a friend always ready to help. Professors, colleagues, friends and workmates like John Nolon, Patrick McWhinney, Larry Susskind, Roger Fisher, David Fairman, Bob Bordone, Anthony Wanis St. John, Kathleen Valley,

John Harutunian, Robert Mnookin, Julio Decaro, Francisco Sánchez, Sarah McKernan, Howard Raiffa, Doug Stone, Oscar Arias, Abraham Chayes, Susan Podziba, Jim Tull, Sheila Heen, Gail Bingham, Paul Uhlig, Frank Sander, John Richardson, Gachi Tapia, Francisco Diez, Miriam Pereyra, Adriana Schiffrin, Aída Frese, Guillermo Reineke, Rob Robinson, David Seibel, Jeff Seul, Steve Reifenberg, Michael Wheeler, Wang Juntao, Tian X Hou, Susan Haxley, Ronald Heifetz, Daniel Sabsay, Sara Horowitz, Daniel Ryan, Paddy López Aufranc, Mónica Moreira, José Sáez, Dolores Padilla, Patty Kistenmacher, José Bercetche, Jorge V. Zagarese, Nico Lucas, Carlos Fierro, José Agote, Marta Galperín, Jorge Narciso, Julio Saguier, Alejandro Massot, Alejandro Litovsky and especially to my partner in Ingouville & Nelson, Patricio Máximo Nelson.

To the memory of Alfredo Olaechea 'El Vasco' and his friends Boy Olmi and Yaco Ansaldo, fantastic storytellers, and their families.

To Glyn Stork, thanks to whom this book is being published in Britain and the US.

To Luis Ingouville who wrote the English version.

To my parents who, although not always on the same side, provided a fascinating stimulus.

To Inés and Tano who, among many other merits, must be credited with introducing me to the stories of Anthony de Mello.

To my sons, Simon and Mateo, whom I admire... although anything I might add here will be incomplete.

And of course Maru Pardo, the main motivation of my daily gratitude.

Francisco Ingouville

Contents

Foreword

Francisco Ingouville studied mediation and negotiation at Harvard University, USA. From his vast experiences, he has produced a book of memories, anecdotes and examples that guide us through the art of negotiation and mediation. This book was originally published in Spanish, and brought to our attention by Glyn Stork, who uses our No Blame/ Support Group approach to bullying in Argentina. Her husband translated the original manuscript into English.

Normally I skim manuscripts, but this book caught my attention and I read every word in one sitting. It's not just a book of memories and anecdotes, it's far more sophisticated. It links experiences and stories into a rich, colourful tapestry that engages the reader in a personal way.

I responded positively to Francisco, but suggested that the book perhaps would benefit from some type of structure, chapters, organising stories into clusters etc.

Francisco replied:

> I am delighted that you liked the stories. I myself enjoyed each one of them when I heard them or read them. I thought they were a good way to spread the idea of win-win negotiations among people who would not be interested in reading an essay on the subject.

> I am sure the book can be improved. In the Spanish version the publishers tried to set the stories in a more orderly way grouping them by subject, but the whole thing lost its freshness… so they finally published it as you saw it.

> I must admit I find it very difficult to classify stories into clusters. Mainly because stories have many meanings and sometimes one can be unfair by limiting its content to a previously set idea.

The book explores the issues of conflicts, the difficulty in resolving disputes and identifies that mediation and negotiation can often offer the best solution.

The book, as well as being a good read, can be used as a stimulus in countless ways:

- To generate discussion
- To support win-win approaches to conflict
- To add colour to mediation training
- To help those in conflict understand their positions
- Stories for assemblies.

We have provided an index for left-brain thinkers but this was a difficult task. We have suggested categories that might represent occasions or problems in your life and grouped the stories in the index that way, hoping that the stories we have suggested can offer help and guidance. You may disagree with our categories so we have also provided a large margin for right-brain thinkers to personalise the book into a structure that suits individual schemas.

The final word should be Francisco's:

> *"Somebody said that when art can be explained it is not necessary."*

Please note:

Some of the anecdotes will be similar to a situation that you have experienced or are experiencing. Others are political or social examples of behaviour that we can identify with. Some of these touch on events that are wrought with tension – for example the Israel-Palestine conflict. Francisco uses these examples not to sensationalise or to trivialise but to showcase difficult attitudes that prevail and go some way towards explaining the prejudice. His commentary about each story supports and contextualises the story.

As publishers, we do not have affiliations with any political or religious groups, nor are we biased towards a certain country, colour of skin, sexuality, gender, level of ability or age. The stories are written to promote thought, and to show that despite dreams of a society where discrimination doesn't exist, it has done and will do. This is why we need mediators.

Hopefully, if we can learn from the examples in this book, we might be able to stop further similar situations from occurring.

George Robinson

The Stories

1. Combs and Tales

It is said experience is a comb one obtains when there is no hair left to comb. I find this especially interesting because I work as a mediator and consultant in negotiations, and in these tasks experience is a key factor.

While I studied mediation and negotiation at Harvard University, I had the opportunity to work as a mediator at Small Claims Courts in the State of Massachusetts. There I was able to verify the importance of practical experience. It is not just the ease and effectiveness it confers, but the way it can set in knowledge acquired through theory, bringing life and strength to it. This is not new. Confucius said, a number of years back, 'I hear and forget. I see and remember. I do and understand.'

As someone interested in conflict resolution and consensus building, I would at times in my studies find some theoretical analyses and mathematical models far too removed from action, and boring to some extent. Yet when our professors blended in a story with theory to drive a point home, bang! adrenalin flowed, enthusiasm and light reappeared. As if the story acted as a liaison between theory and practice, linking the experience of others to my own. Offering a comb to a person not yet bald.

This led me to spend a number of years creating, collecting and adapting related stories from around the world. By stories I mean a vast spectrum of resources that help transfer on experience and give life to theory – real life cases, aphorisms, exercises, fables, jokes and even simple metaphors. A broad variety of literary forms, whose only common denominator is they are intended to improve our ability to interact in negotiations, mediations, consensus decision processes, and all types of arguments. Generally speaking, they are a part of our culture that is assisting humanity in its transition from litigation, in which there are winners and losers, to consensus agreements, in which all parties win.

It is quite possible that the current history of conflict resolution may some day be identified as a transition period towards a less litigating behaviour. Immersed in our own time, we lack the perspective to be certain of this, but one thing is for sure, a great deal of people are striving to bring about a cultural change, and some very positive ideas are sprouting in the fields of psychology, sociology and law. One of the elements in this change is giving the parties a greater participation in conflict resolution, shifting the role of third parties from judges to mediators. The basic assumption is that only the parties involved in a conflict know what is good for them and what is not. It is not the case of replacing the legal system. Laws will continue to provide a framework within which parties can take their conflicts to court if they do not reach a satisfactory agreement. The role of a third party, in this new scheme, is to facilitate communication without the authority a judge would have over them. The following ancient Chinese tale illustrates this point.

2. Two Boys and One Pie

Two boys had received a pie in payment for a job and were trying to agree on how to split it between them. One thing led to another, and soon they were engaged in a violent argument that was stopped by an older neighbour. Once the neighbour understood what the problem was, he explained to the boys that what they needed was an impartial judge, a role he immediately proceeded to adopt. He then brought a knife and cut the pie in two. After carefully examining the two halves he concluded that one half was larger than the other. With the air of an expert professional, he picked up the larger portion and bit off a sizeable chunk. He again compared the two halves but now it was the other half that seemed bigger. Without hesitation he applied the same treatment to the now larger piece. But again the portion that had been too small was now the larger of the two. The two boys, who were still at odds with each other, stood and watched as their halves grew smaller in turns until there was nothing left of them. Yet no one could deny that the neighbour had imparted justice, since each of them had received exactly the same.

For this story to yield its true value we must bear in mind that the share surrendered to an authoritarian third party is not only our piece of the cake. We also lose our right to dialogue, our opportunity to come up with creative solutions, our chance to use our imagination to make the cake bigger before sharing it, and the convenience of making decisions based on our interests and not only on our rights. We miss out on the great pride that comes with feeling that we have solved the problem among ourselves, thus strengthening our relationships and our ability to face future problems together. The way we go about things in a negotiation may help create a feeling of partnership. Some of Roger Fisher's advice may be worthwhile remembering, as in the following story.

3. On the Same Side

In his bestselling book *Getting to Yes*, Roger Fisher recommends that parties in a negotiation sit along the same side of a desk, facing a sheet of paper on which they attempt to describe the problem that brings them together. Thus, they treat each other as partners rather than opponents, they belong to the same team, and they help each other in the search for a solution that can satisfy them both.

During the first round of talks that led to the signing of a peace treaty between Ecuador and Peru, bringing a forty-year-old border conflict to an end, a photographer took several snapshots of Presidents Mahuad and Fujimori chatting across a table. Fisher, who at the time acted as their advisor, asked them if they would do one last photo, this time sitting side by side and analysing the same sheet of paper. This was the photo that was released to the press.

For people in both countries the photograph proved a revelation and set an example. These were people from countries which had lost soldiers during a lasting conflict, people who had heard their politicians deliver fiery speeches lashing out at their enemy and demanding their heads. On this photograph, these same people could now see their leaders working as part of one team, facing a common problem. This got things off to a good start and made it easier for both parties to accept the final solution which, as is common in these cases, had many difficult points to digest for both sides.

Because justice must be just, it is restricted to working with proof, rights and procedures. This may at times, unfortunately and paradoxically, lead to results which are less just and especially much less convenient than what parties could agree upon among themselves. When parties negotiate among themselves, they are aware that they are, to borrow Robert Mnookin's expression, 'Bargaining in the shadow of the law'. If they feel that whatever they are agreeing upon will be a better solution than that offered by a judge, they will not hesitate in closing the deal, saving both time and money. The following story illustrates this point in a very simple way.

4. Conflict at a Restaurant

A fat bearded client at a restaurant calls the waiter and kindly asks him to turn the music volume down, since he cannot stand rock 'n' roll.

'Oh! Sir,' replies the waiter. 'I don't know what to say. Only a minute ago people over at that table asked me to turn the volume up.'

'I insist,' the bearded man says, in a calm but firm voice, barely looking up from the piece of bread he is carefully spreading butter on.

'I'll see what they say,' says the waiter, trying to be diplomatic. He walks over to the other table where, for a while, he can be seen engaging in active talk, only to return a moment later with a somewhat disheartened look about him. The people at the other table are not to be persuaded. They claim they always have either music or the TV on during meals, and as far as they are concerned, they would prefer to have the music even louder.

The waiter comes and goes a couple more times and consults the restaurant owner, who gazes uncomfortably from one table to the other, failing to come up with a way out of this difficult situation.

In the meantime, the scene has drawn the attention of other people at nearby tables. At one of these tables, a judge happens to be having lunch with a mediator. The restaurant owner turns to them for help and gives them a detailed account of the situation. The judge issues his recommendation to the restaurant owner.

'Call the parties together and explain to them; through simple logic they will understand that the music volume cannot be high and low at the same time. There are neither regulations nor established customs that may give us any precise guideline on whether the volume level should be this or that, so one of the two sides will lose and the other side will win. I'll base my decision on the principle of seniority. The first come has the right to choose and the other can either accept or go somewhere else.'

The mediator turns to the restaurant owner. 'The agreement must be based upon their interests. If I understood correctly, what the bearded man cannot stand is rock 'n' roll, whereas the people at the other table couldn't care what type of music is played, they even eat with the TV on. I would ask them if they'd be willing to let the bearded man pick the type of music and let the other table set the volume.'

We have just seen how the new trend focuses on what parties are prepared to accept rather than on any rights they can draw from the past. Obviously this trend works under the assumption that laws exist and that judges will issue their sentences if no agreement is reached. Yet most of the negotiations we carry out daily need not be taken to court. When a family plans what to do for a holiday, or when we discuss a job with a supplier, we wouldn't dream of letting the legal system decide for us, thank God! It is perhaps in these situations, where the attitude of sitting on the same side and looking for a solution that satisfies the needs of all parties reveals its value. And yet it is an attitude we tend to forget in the face of conflict. By and large, the combative attitude makes us concentrate on what is apparently driving us against each other instead of using our imagination to solve the problem that has set us at opposite ends of a conflict. Identifying things we have in common can help us understand that, when one party benefits, the other party also benefits. Then we can go over the differences in our needs, so that each party can hang on to what it is most interested in, in exchange for giving up things that are less of a priority.

The following story carries the virtue of finding opportunities in differences to an extreme that makes it memorable.

5. Five Heroes

On a cool spring morning, a priest, a well-known doctor and a young negotiation professor were out for a game of golf. Although none of them had played that golf course before, they all seemed to be getting on fairly well and managing good scores which, as is common among golfers, kept the party in a cheerful mood. Before long they caught up with the group playing ahead of them and they were forced to wait. Waiting made them lose part of their concentration and, when they were able to continue the game, bad luck had it that one of them hit a tremendous slice, another a horrid pull, and the third one a socket that barely carried the ball a few yards. Golfers are known to be quick to find excuses for their poor performance, and these three proved to be no exception.

'Look at those guys!' the doctor complained. 'They could certainly move a little faster!'

The priest shared the doctor's feeling and stared at the players ahead with an admonishing look, as he slowly shook his head, even though, at such distance, no one could have detected condemnation in his expression.

As he studied the players in the distance, the young professor exclaimed.

'But...can there possibly be five of them?'

And so it was. The golfers ahead of them behaved in a most strange manner, they walked slowly and played poorly, but of all their sins, the one that clearly stood out in open transgression of golf rules was that they were five players, when the maximum allowed is four.

'I'll report this to the golf course captain right away,' said the doctor as he produced a tiny pale-blue mobile phone.

Even before the doctor had put his call through, the priest told his caddy. 'Please go and tell them to give us way immediately or they will face the consequences.'

'But, don't you know who those men are?' a senior caddy then asked respectfully.

'What do you mean, if we know who they are?' replied the doctor, who was prepared to fight any argument that supported privilege.

'Those are the five heroes,' continued the caddy.

'And what exactly does that mean?'

'Of course, you are not members of this club. Three years ago there was a terrible fire in the clubhouse and the children care-centre was engulfed by flames. With the whole building ablaze, those five men fought their way in at the risk of their lives and rescued all the children. In saving the children's lives they suffered burns in their eyes, and all five of them are now blind.'

'Good Heavens!' the priest exclaimed.

The caddy went on. 'In recognition the Club has granted them permission to play as often as they please, all five of them together.'

A moment of remorseful silence followed. The priest was consumed in shame for his initial attitude and his face showed it, but he smiled and admitted that he had learnt his lesson well.

'God has wonderful ways to teach us to be humble. Just a few seconds ago I was acting like a bully,' he broke off, overtaken by his own emotion and then concluded. 'Don't count me in for next Saturday's game, I'll spend the day in penitence, praying for the souls of these good men.'

'How true,' said the doctor. 'I feel the same way. I think I'll offer them my services at no charge. These fellows risked their lives, lost their sight, and all they ask for is to be allowed to play golf together in a course that belongs to them, but they'll never be able to see again. They've shown us a great lesson.'

'Yes,' pondered the negotiation professor, and then he added. 'I also want to help. Perhaps I could give them advice. For example, I'll recommend that they play at night.'

There is a certain touch of cruelty in this story that can overshadow the professor's geniality in discovering benefits for the parties amid their own differences. A good negotiator will first think of ways of making the cake bigger before sharing it. Although I personally love this story, and its dramatic twist contributes to make it spicier, new trends in negotiation are, in contrast, extremely painless, and ever conscious of respect, equanimity and psychological contention. In order to be able to negotiate within the framework of these values, it is recommended that the other negotiating parties also be familiar with them, and feel absolutely committed and determined to be good negotiators in this respect.

I am convinced that, as human beings, our actions are guided by convenience. I am not referring to individual convenience only. We are social beings and complying with certain community rules is part of our nature. We do this for love, to become appreciated members of our community, and for society to be able to function well and provide its members with everything a healthy society can provide. Part of our behaviour is oriented towards satisfying the expectations of the group we belong to. This is perhaps the reason why, when in a strange surrounding, we tend to observe timidly rather than act, until we understand the relationship between people. For social beings, what is actually expected from them bears a remarkable influence on their behaviour. Next I'll tell you about an experiment in social psychology I learnt, which I believe to be a perfect illustration of this point.

6. The Name of the Game

Two groups of people were invited to play a game in two separate rooms. The rules of the game, which were identical for both groups, indicated that each player was on his own, and the winner would be the one who scored most points when the game was over. A certain degree of co-operation between players was an option in the dynamics of the game, but it was left entirely up to the players' judgement. In one of the rooms the name 'Wall Street' was printed in big letters on the game board and box. In the other room, the name on the game board and box was 'Community Game' in the same size print.

The difference was significant. There was no other cause or influence to alter the behaviour of the groups. However, those playing 'Wall Street' were much more aggressive, individualistic and treacherous than those who played the 'Community Game', who behaved in a more considerate, co-operative and selfless way. Individual scores were also higher in the 'Community Game', due to co-operation.

What we colloquially refer to as 'our personality' does not act independently, but is rather a function of the 'game we are playing', in other words, 'the rules which our society has adopted and the compliance expected from us'. In connection with this subject, Robert Putnam, creator of the concept of 'Social Capital', has come up with some interesting discoveries in Italy. Over dinner, he once told a group of Mason Fellows about them. An invaluable story that sums up twenty-five years of research follows.

7. Choirs and Soccer Clubs

Several decades ago in Italy, a number of new municipalities were simultaneously created across the country. Because they originated from the same law, and because their structure and other details were the same in all cases at the starting point, they presented a rare opportunity to study comparative development and evolution. Twenty years later each one of them had evolved in its own style, with varying degrees of effectiveness. Putnam was interested in the quality of the services they offered their "clients", in other words, their citizens. A number of tests were conducted to measure this quality. I remember one of these tests consisted of reporting an address change over the telephone and then counting how many people the call went through before it reached the official in charge of this service, and what was the total time required to conclude the operation. Another test was to request information by mail, and time how long the reply would take.

These tests were carried out throughout the country and the differences encountered were remarkable. What was it that made twin administrations perform so differently? Of all the variables analysed, the number of soccer clubs and choirs per town had the highest correlation with service quality. Putnam goes on to explain that community institutions, as soccer clubs and choirs in this story, reflect a social vocation and provide a setting where individuals relate, not only to other individuals, but also to the community itself. According to Putnam, in communities with a higher frequency of clubs and choirs, members are more likely to do things for others without expecting something directly in return, because they trust they will get something back from the community in the long run. The reverse of this would be a more primitive attitude, typical of a Mafia group or a corrupt system in which one will not give service unless something is offered directly in return.

Whatever the culture, there is a lot that can be done in a community to improve the way in which things are negotiated or the way in which decisions are made among two or more parties. Perhaps the most important thing is to know clearly what one wants. I am often reminded of this by a story told to me by my friend Paul Uhlig, a doctor who always has a tale full of wisdom to share.

8. How to Plough in a Straight Line

Paul and his father had their life-long dream come true the day they managed to buy a small farm in Kansas. They had never farmed before, so they had no choice but to learn as they went along. They purchased a used tractor and beamed with excitement as they started working their own land for the first time. As they reached the far end of the field and turned to admire their work they were shocked to see the most crooked thing ever to be named a furrow in the State of Kansas. For a while they stared at each other in puzzlement and then decided they would have a second go and try and do better. But it turned out just as bad, and their third attempt was even worse. At this point they drove the tractor to a halt in midfield and got off, their hearts sinking. They were scratching their heads in search of an answer when a neighbour appeared in the distance, walking towards them. He was an elderly man with a small-framed body, who limped as farmers often do, come a certain age. He eventually caught up with them and they exchanged greetings. As customary, they discussed the weather for a while, then talked about the wheat they were going to plant, and finally got down to their worries about their sinewy ploughing. Paul thought the neighbour was probably too polite to bring up the subject, but he surely must feel embarrassed to have such a poorly worked field next to his beautiful farm. Finally, they asked him for advice.

For a moment the old farmer glanced at them and then he suggested they turn off the tractor and follow him. He took a few steps away from where they had been standing and raised one arm pointing at the horizon.

'What do you see over there?' he asked.

'Nothing,' said Paul and then, seeing that his reply would not be satisfactory, he added meekly. 'A tree stump.'

'That's no stump,' said the old man. 'It's a landmark. Once you find one on the horizon, you raise your eyes over the field and the dust and fix them on it. It becomes your objective. If you drive your tractor aiming at your objective you'll plough the straightest furrows no one's ever seen.'

So Paul and his father tried it this way and saw it was true.

Paul ends his story with a smile, and the look in his eyes reveals that the old farmer's advice has given him a lot more than straight furrows.

Each time I go back over this story I discover new meanings. It could be said that goal-setting is the ABC of planning. But even the most experienced negotiators admit that the dust raised by their ploughs has distracted them more than once.

It is also true that in a consumer society, where we tend to associate 'more' with 'better', goal-setting acquires an added importance, as it keeps us from an insane chase beyond what is necessary.

Mental laziness can interfere with setting objectives. Setting objectives is undoubtedly no easy task and sometimes touches upon subjects we would rather not face. Answering questions like, 'What do I want?' and, 'Why do I want this?' may imply an inward search we may not be ready for. However, it seems far more convenient to go through this self-analysis prior to negotiating than to start a negotiation with unclear answers. In his book *Alice in Wonderland*, Lewis Carroll touches upon this subject when Alice has the following conversation with the Cheshire Cat:

'Would you tell me please, which way I ought to go from here?' Alice said.

'That depends a good deal on where you want to go,' said the Cheshire Cat.

'I don't much care where,' said Alice.

'Then it doesn't matter which way you go,' said the Cat.

The following popular saying, from an anonymous source, also relates to this issue: 'If you don't know what you are looking for you won't understand what you find.' I often come across cases in which, rather than performing a self-analysis, people find it easier to set false goals based on the effect those goals might have on others.

> If a man were asking a price of $1000 for his car, I would be very satisfied if, after a 'skillful' negotiation, I managed to close the deal for $800, and also noticed the man was not too happy with what he got. If I acted this way, I would not be basing my goal-setting on my own interests but on other reasons. In other words, I would be driven to action by motives I had not carefully considered. Two old stories give us examples on this.

9. The Lost Ring

> That night Franz had lost a ring along the side of the road and was anxiously searching the ground around the spot of light provided by a lamp post. Fritz turned up and, no sooner he learned what had happened, got down on his knees and joined his friend in the search.
>
> 'Franz, are you sure this is where you lost the ring?' Fritz asked, after half an hour of fruitless ground combing.
>
> 'No Fritz,' replied Franz. 'In fact I'm quite certain I lost it over by that tree there.'
>
> 'What do you mean? How come you are looking for it here then?'

'Well, it doesn't take much brains to see you'd never find anything under a tree where it's dark, whereas here we have a splendid street lamp!'

In situations where envy or competition is involved, our motives may be even more tangled up, as in the following story.

10. The Wish

A farmer once found a bottle by the river and asked his neighbour to keep it for him until he returned from the market. When the farmer had gone, the neighbour uncorked the bottle to check its contents, and possibly steal a few sips without the farmer noticing. But as he proceeded to do this, a genie emerged from the bottle, claiming he had been trapped in there for centuries. The genie was anxious to return to his remote land but also felt grateful and would grant one wish to the farmer who had uncorked the bottle, and two wishes to the one who had recovered it from the river.

'The man who rescued the bottle has gone to the market and will not be back till nightfall,' said the neighbour.

'A stroke of bad luck!' said the genie. 'I wouldn't want to wait that long. Make your wish, then, and I will grant your neighbour twice as much as you ask for.'

The farmer considered the situation. Whatever wishes came to mind lost all attraction when he realized his neighbour would belittle him by receiving double. If he asked for the best horse in the county, his neighbour would have two horses as magnificent as his, and he would become a mere second to him. If he asked for more land he would be no better off. Whatever wishes he thought of would render him poorer than his neighbour. His tribulations went on until the genie could wait no longer and pressed.

'Name your wish now or you'll be left without one!'

'Very well,' said the farmer. 'My mind is made up. Make me blind in one eye.'

Conflicts are likely to take hold of the negotiator's mind to the point that defeating the opponent may become the one and only goal. As a result, the winner may find himself empty-handed and without a partner with whom to spar with. The farmer in this next story may not represent all of us, but let us take a look at how people behave in a social psychology experiment which addresses a similar problem.

11. Self-appraisal and Ultimatum

A social psychology experiment carried out by postgraduate students of a business school consisted of a negotiation exercise in which the discussion was over a price. The students were told some of them would compete against other students from the same university, and some would compete against students from some distant university. None would get to see their opponents and their communication would be anonymous, by written mail. Actually all responses were managed by the team that conducted the experiment, and the competitors did not exist. At the end of the test they were asked to fill out a self-appraisal form describing how they felt about the results of the negotiation. In other words, if they had more or less achieved what they expected, if they thought they had handled the process skilfully, and how the results had affected their feelings.

Some of the students were allowed to see the self-appraisals of their 'opponents' (which were fake, created by the investigators) before they went on to fill out their own self-appraisal forms. In other words, they believed they were reading about how their opponents felt regarding the results of the negotiation they had just concluded. There were three types of responses of the phony opponents.

Very good (I feel exceedingly satisfied, I got more than I expected).

Satisfactory (the result is more or less what I expected).

Unsatisfactory (I achieved much less than I had anticipated).

Although the self-appraisals were varied, the investigators had manipulated the results so that all participants ended up obtaining the same points or monetary result.

While working on their self-appraisals, participants were widely influenced by what their 'competitors' had expressed. In those cases where the 'competitors' had appraised their performance as very good, their own rating of negotiating ability was poor. However, they were careful to point out their own generosity, kindness, understanding, politeness, and other social graces. In other words, they had a positive rating for their affective components and a negative rating for their intellectual components. Likewise, when the 'competitors' expressed they had done poorly in the negotiation, participants claimed to have operated skilfully and intelligently, although in a greedy, ambitious and unkind manner.

As the next step in the experiment, participants had to go through an exercise called 'Ultimatum', interacting with the same 'supposed' opponents as before. In this exercise participants were given each

$10 and told they would have to share them with their opponent (who was out of sight, in another room). Participants were free to offer to share any proportion of the money. The 'opponent' could only accept or turn down the offer. If the offer were turned down, neither side would receive any money. If the offer were accepted, each one would take the agreed amount.

Those participants whose 'opponents' in the previous negotiation had complained that they had done poorly offered sums considerably larger, as if they intended to compensate. This happened in those cases in which the 'opponents' were supposedly members of the same university. It did not happen in cases where the 'opponents' belonged to a distant university.

If asked to do a self-appraisal, it is only natural that we take into account the effect our interaction with another person has had on that person. Adjectives and the language itself are entirely social elements. Yet no one can deny that when we suffer cold, hunger or pain, we do so individually. This means an internal negotiation takes place between individual and social needs.

There is a traditional debate on how much of a human being is derived from nature and how much from its social environment. This is the dilemma on 'Nature' and 'Nurture' which Jean Claude Filoux refers to in his book *Personality*. When we talk about negotiation, some people argue that what one essentially is cannot be changed. Those who believe in the unyielding designs of genetics prefer the following ancient tale.

12. The Scorpion and the Frog

A scorpion that wished to cross a river asked a frog if he would carry him across on his back.

'The strength of your poison is well known,' replied the frog. 'Only a fool would let you on his back.'

'You are dumber than you look,' the scorpion retorted. 'Can't you see that if I were to sting you, I'd end up drowning myself?'

The frog blushed in embarrassment at his own foolish reasoning and uneasily accepted the scorpion's request. He let the scorpion climb on his back and pushed off towards the other shore.

They were already halfway across when the frog suddenly felt a fierce sting on his back, followed by the unmistakable, paralysing pain caused by poison. 'Now you'll drown too. What did you do that for?' he managed to cry, as strength abandoned him.

'I couldn't help it,' answered the scorpion. 'It's my nature.'

I am mortified by the tale of the scorpion. I rebel against that part of it which seems to proclaim, "Don't bother to plan, learn or teach. In the long run, our malign essence will prevail". Still the story appeals to me because of its shocking dramatic effect and because it definitely singles out the issue we should tackle. Next is a real life story once told to me by Stan Christensen.

13. Father and Son

A friend of Stan's had a six-year-old son who never ceased to ask for sweets, ice cream, toys, and to be taken to the movies. The boy was very demanding and his manner was irritating. This went on until one day the father approached his son wearily. 'You have no idea how exhausting your attitude can be. You should try to put yourself in my shoes to see how it feels.' Then, out of impulse, he decided to go through with his idea and show the boy what it was like. 'I'll be the son and you'll be the father,' he said. He then crouched to make himself shorter and began begging for all sorts of things. He wanted to be taken to the movies, and on the way out could he buy him some toys, could he have an ice cream and then go to an amusement park. While he was actively playing the spoiled son's part the father was suddenly struck by the thought that the boy might very well reply 'OK, let's go, let's do all that right now!' So the father would have fallen into his own trap.

The boy did nothing of the sort, but stared at his father.

'You be quiet and go to your room right now,' he said sternly.

The opportunity to dominate and punish his father appealed more to the boy than his favourite programme. This gave the father much food for thought.

Any resemblance to the tale of the scorpion? Was the boy's nature to blame, or was it the way he had been brought up? According to Filoux it is the result of a particular dialogue between these two elements that stretches back to the beginning of the boy's life.

The following is another real life story, which takes us back on a more optimistic path and shows a pattern of nature in deep contrast with that of the scorpion. It sets the type of example that, were it to spread among society, would make win-win negotiations easier to achieve.

14. Sharing the Wind

For years biologists had wondered in admiration how Emperor Penguins could survive South Pole climatic conditions which are, as a rule, unbearably bitter, and can at times turn harsh enough to stamp out any form of life on Earth. Needless to say, the temperatures are among the lowest in the world, often magnified by a chill factor from winds blowing at over 120 kilometres per hour.

In recent observations it was found that, at times like these, the penguins join together and slowly walk around in a circle. In this way, those most exposed to the wind are constantly being replaced by others, and none of them are exposed for too long. The time each one is exposed is compensated by a longer time behind the shelter of the others, and that gives them a chance to recover.

What makes individuals trust each other and work in solidarity as in this case? Perhaps some answers can be found in our cultural heritage wrapped in stories of life and behaviour. I am particularly drawn by stories which present different approaches to the relationship between individuals and their communities, or among community members themselves. Here is a story that depicts our darker side.

15. The Other Guy

Nathan walked into a bar where he usually met with his friends. He had one arm in a cast, a missing tooth, and a half-shut, swollen eye. His friends had already heard of the fistfight of the night before and wasted no time making fun of him, and coming up with all sorts of smart remarks that had everyone else roaring with laughter. Nathan had expected this. He resisted patiently and waited for all to fall silent before he presented his line of defence.

'Any of you seen what's left of the other guy?'

Was the other guy's condition important at all? Let's not kid ourselves. It is easy to ridicule Nathan and say the other guy's condition will not bring relief to his blackened eye, and we are probably right. But there are other rewards involved, like social prestige, authority and fame. In some cases there may be an unspoken social agreement whereby authority must be acquired by fighting. Sometimes we are not fighting strictly over the motive that initially triggered off the conflict. The fight is to establish authority, the motive a mere excuse.

16. The Arm Wrestle

During his seminars, Roger Fisher will often ask the audience to find partners and hold hands as in an arm wrestle. The objective, he explains, is to push the partner's arm until the back of his hand touches the table, which scores one point. Each player must try to score as many points as possible, disregarding the partner's score. Usually, the strongest partners in each team will score between 2 and 8 points in a minute, and will sometimes, out of mercy, let their partner score the odd point.

Those who already know the game, or are sufficiently open-minded to listen and make the most of the rules of the game, manage to score about 60 points each. All they do is swing their arms back and forth as fast as they can in the manner of a pendulum gone wild, neither partner offering resistance. Why offer resistance if our partner's score makes no difference to us? By co-operating with our partners we receive, in return, the co-operation we need.

It is said the dog guarding the vegetable garden neither eats nor allows others to eat the food he so fiercely defends. But this dog is at least rewarded by its owner with loving care. What does the arm wrestler stand to gain if he will not score nor let his opponent score either?

At first sight, out of these two stories, the example to follow is that of the arm wrestlers who agree to swing their arms back and forth quickly, paying no attention to their partner's score. At the opposite end is the man with the blackened eye, for whom the damage he has caused his opponent is more important than his own bruises and missing tooth. The choice seems obvious, yet we do not always get it right. Could it possibly be spite? There must be an underlying motive undetected at first glance. If co-operating is so easy and advantageous, why not do it each time?

Why are so many sports based on competition? I do not think I would be very much off target if I claimed sports are a life drill which allows us to rehearse our role in what we will later on have to face. In some cases, like mountain climbing, nature levies such a burden of adversity a human rival is rendered unnecessary. But clearly we seek hard challenge in sport. I can't help associating this concept with the idea of vaccination, which introduces low rates of diluted 'adversity' in our bodies to force our immune system to fight back and be prepared. Probably many of the conflicts we become involved in have this 'immuno-stimulating' function. In a context of natural selection of the species it is not surprising that those of us who are alive have a tendency to search for ways of being prepared to survive any situation. The great majority of conflicts are not deadly. 'What doesn't kill you makes you stronger', in other words, it will provide us with the skills needed to survive. Conflicts are often a stimulus for change and the creation of a new status quo.

It is useful to remember that what we fight over is not always the real motive for the fight. There can be other motives, for example establishing a hierarchy. Fistfights and other conflicts are often triggered off by some minor excuse, and provide a means to establish who will give and who will take orders in the future. Establishing territorial boundaries, extending them, or even preventing someone from expanding their boundaries at our expense may be the real stakes in a fight. In a chicken coop a pecking order is established through continual fighting. And some human organisations show a remarkable resemblance to a chicken coop. We are perfectly able to find organisational systems which are more developed than the one prevailing in chicken coops, but it may be worthwhile to be aware that such alternatives exist among human beings. I went through an experience that was quite excruciating once.

17. Useful Defeat

During a year I spent in military service I was once driven into a fistfight with a heavier and taller soldier to establish our pecking order.

Early each morning at the barracks the corporal would stomp into the dormitory where two hundred of us slept, blowing energetically on his whistle. With a jolt every soldier would stand at attention, toeing a yellow line painted on the floor along the edges of the cots, next to which we had carefully lined our boots and socks the night before. We would stand there in our underwear until the corporal would yell his next order, 'Get dressed!', at which we would hastily slip on our shirts, pants, socks and boots. We had five minutes to be in formation, ready to march to the Arms Plaza.

This one day, when the order to get dressed was heard, the soldier to my left mumbled something like, 'I'm missing a sock' and, without hesitation, picked up one of mine. Half asleep, rushed, and taken off guard, I failed to react, yet felt that something bad had just started to happen to me. Like Hamlet, I was confronted with the question to be or not to be, over a cotton sock. Whether to accept this open violation and submit to this soldier's authority, or to challenge him and suffer the likely consequences of his 15-kilo advantage. The problem haunted my mind throughout the morning. Time and again I wished the incident had never happened, but there was no question it had. The moment of decision is lonely and excruciating. Finally I made up my mind to face him.

As I considered my strategy, I thought I should choose a crowded place for the fight where nearby people would hopefully disengage us before this heavyweight butchered me. If I let him get too close, I would be no match for his strength, and at a distance I would be at the mercy of his longer reach. It was noon by the time I made the decision and digesting lunch was agony.

Back in the dormitory I found him, casually sprawled on my bunk, reading a magazine. Although it was quite usual for soldiers to lie on any bunk during free time, I saw this as an opportunity and tersely ordered him off my bed. The few others around us looked up in puzzled amazement and the giant shot a scornful laugh at me. He was still laughing when I punched him squarely on the side of his head. He was startled by the blow and seemed to hesitate for a moment, but he reacted and in a flash he was on his feet charging towards me, while I quickly lost the advantage of having been the first to strike.

I did my best in sticking to my plan and not getting too hurt, and soon after the fight was broken up. I was thrilled to see him put up little resistance when his roommates held him back. And I was grateful he never hunted me down to pick up where we'd left. From that day on I felt his respect for me had grown, and he eventually sought my friendship.

That soldier knew he could beat me, but every fight entails some risk and, above all, an exertion we generally prefer to avoid. Many animal species have rituals and shows of strength they put on to avoid fighting. I succeeded in stopping a bully by staging a fight that ended up more like a show of strength by primates. I didn't win, I scarcely managed to inflict any damage, but I made it clear that I was willing to take the risk. Being prepared to accept defeat can be useful if the opponent is not keen on entering the fight.

A foolish game called 'chicken', played by unbalanced teenagers in the United States some decades ago, brutally exposes the elements in this problem.

18. Chicken

In this 'game' two cars drive towards each other at high speed from opposite ends of a single lane. The first one to veer off loses and is considered a chicken. Which possible outcome could make them both winners? Hideous thoughts come to mind.

The only thing a competitor can do to win is to try to scare his opponent. He must convincingly pretend he is willing to commit suicide. He might as well tear the steering wheel off and daringly wave it outside the car window at the opponent to add to his intimidating act. Ironically, deliberately limiting our freedom of action can drive us to victory.

Brandishing a steering wheel taken off any other car would do the trick. In other words, it is enough for the opponent to be convinced that the oncoming car cannot be steered off the road.

This is not the type of 'game' I look forward to in my present work. I have often wondered how I would handle the incident with the soldier today, twenty-five years later, a lot of them spent on mediation and negotiation. Coincidentally, I was destined to participate in a situation which bears some similarities to the sock conflict. This time I was at the opposite end of the table, advising Roque Sevilla, Mayor of Quito, in a negotiation with informal street vendors.

19. The Street Vendors of Quito's Historical Centre

When Quito's Historical Centre was proclaimed 'World Heritage', several projects were drawn up to resettle next to ten thousand street vendors whose stalls lined the old town's streets, often haphazardly nailed against the ancient walls of historical buildings. In Lima, a similar process had led to an all-out bloody battle between merchants and police. The news quickly spread and made the front pages of major newspapers around the globe.

The mayor of Quito wanted a peaceful and negotiated settlement, and I was hired to train and advise government officials in charge of conducting negotiations with the street vendors. The government officials' task was no picnic. The street vendors had informal organisational structures and leaders among which violence, threats, blackmail, bribery, and other actions usually associated with Mafia groups, were daily occurrences.

A team of government architects was busy designing a number of shopping centres at which street vendors would be able to purchase stores at subsidised prices and on long-term loans. Nevertheless, the street vendors opposed to the project. Under the guidance of various leaders who competed endlessly among themselves, they objected to the prices and the deadlines. They stuck to the rights they claimed to have acquired over years of occupying the very same public space they were now being evicted from.

The negotiating team had been trained to shift from positions to interests, and very successfully developed options that might prove satisfactory to the vendors. They were even willing to lower the price. Yet a deep worry consumed them. The street vendors could easily accept the concessions made by the government, and then refuse to comply with the resettlement programme, coming back with new demands.

Come to that, the government's only resort would be to enforce eviction. Both the government and the street vendors were well aware that the use of force would politically damage the Mayor. If troops were sent in, the street vendors knew it would mean a physical defeat but a political triumph to them. Women, children and elderly people of low-income families clobbered by police officers would make an ugly sight to be avoided at any cost. Yet, however undesirable the scene, it added to the street vendors' negotiating power. In fact, they could sit back and delay talks at a minimum risk.

The situation reminded me of my useful defeat at the military service. If the vendors clashed with police forces, the ensuing political upheaval would weaken the government's position. After that, it would be increasingly difficult to carry the project through. The church, the police, the politicians, public opinion, opposition parties, human rights organisations, development organisations, neighbours, commercial banks, shop owners, and international banks which supported the project, in other words, just about everybody that mattered, would begin to wonder whether things were being properly handled. This would give the street vendors a chance to get away without honouring their part of the deal. Hence the government's reluctance to go ahead with the options they had developed to satisfy vendors' needs, let alone the reduction in the price of new stores.

All things considered, the path we chose to follow was to invite all the mentioned sectors, including the street vendors, to a meeting. The object of the meeting was to decide, with the help of mediators, what ethical values the negotiation with the street vendors should be based upon. This allowed room for reflection and made the street vendors feel they were being considered and respected by the rest. It was no longer a question of making impossible demands to bog down the negotiation. Unbiased people were listening. Proposals had to be serious and moderate. The level of commitment to comply with the terms of any agreement reached was increased on both sides. As of that moment, the vendors' leaders were aware that, if they fell short on their word and failed to do their share of the deal once their demands had been met, the use of force would no longer be regarded as unjust abuse by leading members of the community. Emotional and political blackmail would not be as easy to get away with. If the government kept its promises the vendors would be forced to follow suit. Even seeking to be defeated by police forces would prove less useful. The seed had been planted and the resettlement was finally carried out peacefully.

The Quito process went on for several months. Although my job only covered the initial stages, I made great friends with Monica Moreira, who was in charge of most of the negotiation and did a brilliant job. Each time I received news of the progress they made I felt proud to have been a part of a team that succeeded in avoiding violence.

I believe following ideals implies choosing how we would like to behave and what things make us proud. In my earlier days I was proud to have stood up to a soldier bigger than I was. The next story goes a little deeper into this.

20. The Samurai's Sons

A samurai came across an old comrade, whom he had not seen for many years.

'How has your life been?' he asked him.

'I have travelled many lands and taught the art of the sword,' replied the newcomer. 'How about you?'

'I have taught it too, all my life, yet I stayed back in our home town, I married and had three sons.'

'Congratulations! Will they also become masters of the sword?'

'I am teaching them. Join us for dinner tonight and I will introduce them to you.'

When the guest arrived, the host showed him into the house and placed a bucket full of water over the door that led to his sons' quarters. They both sat down and the father summoned his eldest son.

The youth perceived an unfamiliar weight on the doorknob, cautiously opened the door barely enough to let his hand squeeze through, and caught hold of the bucket. He slid into the room, and after closing the door behind him, replaced the bucket where he had found it.

'This is my eldest son,' said the host. 'He is on the path of the samurai.' He then called in his second son.

The door swung open and the bucket toppled over, but the boy reacted like a flash and caught it midair, spilling only a couple of drops. He then placed the bucket back over the door, and proceeded to sit with the rest.

'This is my second son,' said the host. 'He is on the path of the samurai.'

The third son barged in the moment he was called in and, as a splash of water soaked his head, he drew his sword and split the bucket in half before it hit the floor.

He then went on to sit with the others.

'This is my youngest son,' the father said. 'He's still too young.'

Now the time seems ripe to tell my favourite story. The reader may find my passion for it out of proportion but, when it comes to preferences, I think we all have the right to a small quota of delusion.

The orange story is, in my opinion, the substructural myth of win-win negotiation. Perhaps I ought to have started this book with the phrase. 'In the beginning there was an orange.' So many generations after an apple led us from the Garden of Eden to a world immersed in conflict, the orange mercifully lends us a new tool to survive in that world. When I try to explain to someone what it is I do, I will without fail start with the orange. Next to this, the orange's juice and vitamin C are set aside as lesser virtues.

The story is included in Roger Fisher's book *Getting to Yes*, in which he stresses the importance of distinguishing between positions and interests. Positions are what negotiators say they want. Interests are the reasons why they want what they want.

21. The Orange

Two girls were having a heated argument over an orange until their mother, alerted by their yelling and screaming, broke up the fight.

'What's going on?' she asked.

'I want that orange!' cried one of the girls.

'Me too!' the other one snapped back.

'Very well,' said the mother. She 'Solomonically' split the orange in two and gave each girl a half.

Both girls peeled their halves. One of them ate the pulp and discarded the skin. The other girl threw away the pulp and kept the skin to make marmalade.

The mother had not gone wrong. She had put an end to some very loud and disturbing bickering; she had stopped the fight, and had justly given the girls a part of what they wanted. Yet, had she inquired about their interests instead of working on their positions, each girl could have received double the share.

And all she needed to do was ask, 'Why?, or, 'What for?' in order to shift from positions to interests.

'Not a bad story,' people will often say to me. 'But I deal with problems that are bigger and more complex than oranges. How do you apply this to a labour union conflict or to hard sell bargaining?'

Obviously, if problems were always simple there would be no need for this discussion. Yet the orange story clearly points out the advantages of distinguishing between what people say they want and why they want it, and what they want it for. At every negotiation course I give, I ask the audience to think of examples of hopelessly opposed positions. They don't find this too hard. I then ask for an example of hopelessly opposed interests, and they discover that they are much less frequent. In the last story, even if both girls had wanted to eat the orange, we could take a step further and define their interest as, 'I want to eat something I like', and it is not in the interest of either girl that the other one does not eat something she likes. Nor is that particular orange the only means to satisfy those needs.

The coming stories show how, through a well-conducted negotiation process, people can discover common interests where all they could see initially was conflict.

I have to admit that the orange story is somewhat simple. But I should also warn those who look down on its extreme simplicity that there are stories that are simpler still. For example, next is a masterpiece in simplicity which shows how, from an early age, women tend to be more conciliatory and more considerate of the interests of others.

22. Children at Play

Girl: 'Shall we play neighbours?'

Boy: 'No! I want to play pirates.'

Girl: 'OK, you'll be the pirate who lived next door.'

Next is a real life case which shows how a practical application can be squeezed out of the orange story.

23. The German Trainee

A German student worked as a trainee in a London chemical company. For a small salary, she was an assistant to an engineer who was in charge of certain routine analyses. The engineer suddenly took ill and died some days later. Once the initial shock was over, the girl managed to continue the job on her own. After some time she realised the engineer would not be replaced, as she was efficiently coping with the work. Eventually she approached the manager for a pay raise. Despite her pleas and arguments she got a flat no. When she insisted on more money, the manager stuck to his refusal, and the relationship noticeably worsened.

The manager argued the working hours had not increased, that they had a prearranged agreement, and that this experience would be good for her and would enhance her CV.

She in turn claimed the company was saving the engineer's salary thanks to her, while she had more responsibility and more work to do.

A mediator was called in. He asked her why she wanted more money. He listened carefully to her answers and encouraged her to expand. During their meetings the girl mentioned in passing that she found it very expensive to live in a hostel and fly to Berlin for the weekends to see her boyfriend. She also said she resented the company's lack of recognition towards her.

In private, the manager mentioned that, due to a tight budget, he was under strict orders not to issue any salary raises or hire new staff for one year. Complying with these instructions would have a strong bearing on his personal year-end appraisal.

The mediator asked both of them to communicate these interests mutually, and then they moved on to search for alternative solutions. It so happened the manager was in a position to offer the trainee airline tickets at no charge. The company also owned apartments which were vacant at the time and could be occupied for free by the trainee, at a much greater comfort than the hostel could provide.

By finding alternate ways, they had gone from fighting for positions to satisfying needs.

As a spin-off of their new agreement they made plans to improve the lab's performance, for which the manager would receive recognition, and the trainee would have a stable and better paid job.

The first time I heard the story of the orange split in two I was reminded of the biblical story of King Solomon my father had told me as a boy. He used to refer to wise and just decisions as 'Solomonic' decisions. When my curiosity led me to ask him about the meaning of this word, he explained by telling me the story.

24. King Solomon

Two women were engaged in a fiery dispute over a baby they both claimed as their own. They were led before the King so that he would settle the conflict, given his famous wisdom and justice. Seeing that it was impossible to bring the women to reason, he dictated that, unless an agreement was reached, he would be left no choice but to have the baby cut in two. One of the women sprang forward as if she'd been dipped in boiling water. Crying in desperation she conceded to let the other woman keep the baby. King Solomon then knew her to be the true mother and decreed she should have the child.

Wisdom in this case lies in recognising the nature of a mother, who will tend to protect her child above all. King Solomon acts as a detective (and finally as a judge) rather than as a mediator. Although the story still appeals to me for its ingenuity, I am saddened by the concentration of power which burdens the King. Poor soul, I think to myself, despite being a monarch, he is stuck with having to handle affairs for others.

I look up to a society in which citizens assume responsibility to handle their own conflicts and do not depend on decisions made by others. However, assistance from a third party is useful because otherwise parties find it hard to supervise the process and fight for their interests at the same time. But the participation of a third party must be limited to operating the way traffic lights do. In other words, it must direct the traffic, but not drive cars or tell people which way to go.

25. The Tailor

This is from a comic strip in *La Codorniz*, a Spanish magazine which has long since been discontinued.

A man trying on a tailor-made suit is shocked to discover the jacket has three sleeves. He turns to the tailor in puzzled indignation. The tailor shrugs and then mumbles, with a certain air of indifference, 'Well, since you never specified...'

What is obvious to some, is not so to others. Hence a golden rule of negotiators is 'Check your assumptions', and another rule is, 'Listen attentively and explicitly show you are listening'. Many conflicts are brought about by misunderstandings and lack of communication. It is desirable that negotiators, facilitators and mediators bear this in mind. Efforts to improve communications will reduce the chances of conflict. People tend to find it easier to blame a conflict on poor communications than blame themselves. They would rather base a change of attitude on a motive than change for no apparent reason, and be seen like they were the cause of delays in reaching the agreement. The motive for this change can be learning something which had not been clarified before.

In *Getting to Yes*, Roger Fisher tells us about a friend of his who called the family surgeon in the middle of the night.

26. Appendicitis

'Doctor, I'm sorry to call so late. I suspect my wife has a case of appendicitis. Could we see you at the clinic in half an hour?'

'No, just give her some aspirin and try to get her to sleep.'

'Sleep? Look, I'm not a doctor, but I've seen appendicitis before, and this looks like a typical case to me.'

'No, don't worry. As I said, aspirin, and both of you try to get some sleep.'

'But, I'm really worried, Doctor, how come you are not worried?'

'You see, I performed an appendicitis operation on your wife five years ago, and no woman has a second appendix.'

'That's true, no woman has a second appendix, but some men have a second wife.

Please meet us at the clinic in half an hour.'

Based on my professional knowledge, and knowing the other person to be a layman, I might never even consider looking at the problem from another angle. And when it comes to feelings, it becomes harder than dealing with appendicitis.

Whatever the effort made to understand the other party during a negotiation, it will never be too much. Perhaps both parties have lived through the same situation but have interpreted it differently. We know this happens, but there is nothing like going through a real situation to get a better picture. Bob Bordone, an Instructor at Harvard University's Negotiation Seminar, has a special exercise for this.

27. Interpretation

In this exercise Bob would ask us to take a sheet of paper and close our eyes. He would then give us instructions, but we were not allowed to ask questions or talk between us. He asked us to fold the pages and then fold them again. Next we were asked to cut off a corner and then another. Finally he would ask us to open our eyes and show our results. Although we had all received the same set of instructions, at the same time and place, no two pages were shaped alike.

His moral was, 'Use questions to clarify what you hear. Never take for granted that you have understood correctly'.

Listening to people is, in theory, quite simple, yet we often fail to listen. Our mind is frequently carried away while the other person speaks and, instead of concentrating on understanding what we are being told, we do several other things at the same time.

My colleagues Doug Stone and Sheila Heen, joint authors, together with Bruce Patton, of *Difficult Conversations*, put on an interesting show at a negotiation workshop.

28. Two Voices

Doug and Sheila walk into the classroom and both start addressing the audience simultaneously. However, they are not saying the same thing. The bits of each speech I manage to grasp seem interesting, but obviously it is hard to maintain any form of concentration. As soon as I start following one of then, the other strives to capture my attention and I am lost. There are a few smiles in the audience. A person next to me whispers, 'I think they are trying to tell us something.'

Once they have made sure we are totally baffled and frustrated, they stop their speeches and they take turns to explain what has just happened to us. The theory behind this is when we are listening to someone, we are often listening to our own inner voice at the same time, which contradicts, assesses, refutes, insults and complains. Doug and Sheila have made us see how hard it is to listen when a second voice is interfering.

I believe our inner voice is necessary for survival. If we allowed all messages in, without putting them through some sort of filter, in other words, without analysing, criticising, digesting, classifying, or defending ourselves from them, we would not be persons but formless beings. Or perhaps we would die from over-exposure in a short time. Yet I think it is important to be aware that our inner voice has a specific function, and it should not interfere with our listening to others. And it should definitely allow us to make the other person feel we are giving her our full attention. On this subject, one could not go wrong by overdoing.

When co-ordinating a negotiation workshop, I usually ask the participants to think of someone who is not good at listening. Someone they know well, who has a tendency to interrupt, or to become distracted or unreceptive. I then ask if they consider this person to be trustworthy. The answer is generally no. How could we trust someone who will not take that first step which is getting to know our needs?

In the past I was not very good at listening, which is why I find it one of the most interesting topics in this profession. Those of us who are not blessed with a calm and patient nature have a lot to learn. And once we manage to develop the art of listening there are generous rewards. The prize for patience is patience itself. With patience comes a bonus which is a great opportunity to get to know the other party. We may often find that this attitude catches on, and then the other party is better disposed to listening to us. To clarify this concept, I've developed an analogy, which I display during my workshops.

29. The Fishbowl

In my mediation courses I ask participants to pretend for a moment that the head is a fishbowl, and I draw this as a diagram on the blackboard.

I then go on to explain that, at the slightest sign of conflict, people's heads fill up with water. Water symbolises people's annoyance, their fears, their need to be proved right, their search for understanding. In conflict, the ear level is covered with water, which makes listening impossible. Next I suggest we politely pay attention to others as they speak. They feel reassured and encouraged to continue speaking. As they unload, the level of water goes down.

We are not required to agree with the speaker but it is important that we understand what she is saying and show that we understand. Once the speaker has off-loaded what she wanted to say the water level drops below the ears and she is able to listen.

Usually the first water to come out has 'low nutritional value', in other words, big issues are reserved for later. Only after verifying the other party's trustworthiness will a person risk telling her motives and interests. If we turn out to be good listeners, and we know to keep quiet when we have to, the time may come (generally after an emotional pause) when a small fish will come out with the water. The small fish symbolises the essence of the speaker's interests or personal motivation behind rational argument. This is what we must and need to reply to. Any other efforts to refute positions will be less fruitful.

A sign on the entrance of a Subway station reads, 'Let other passengers get off before you get on'. It is basically the same idea. Once we have grasped this concept it becomes easier to realize the importance of listening. Doug Stone tells a real life story whose simplicity and acuteness help me keep in mind that above all, I should listen.

30. I Want Out

One day on which Doug was holding an important telephone conversation, his young nephew came up to him and told him he wanted to go out. He did not want to interrupt the call or lose concentration, so he pretended not to have heard his nephew, hoping the boy would become dissuaded. However, the little nephew was not to be put off so easily.

'I want to go outside, Doug!'

Doug tried frowning to make the boy understand that he did not want to be interrupted. Yet his signal was completely ineffective.

'Doug! Doug! I want to go outside!'

Doug was forced to cover the mouthpiece for a second. 'I am on the phone!' he whispered with a threatening frown.

The child seemed deaf, blind, but not in the least dumb.

'Doug! Let's go outside! Doug! Doug!'

The situation was becoming unbearable. Doug finally asked the person on the other end of the line to hold for a minute and, staring at his nephew in the eyes, he patiently asked.

'What's the matter?'

'I want to go outside.'

'You want to go outside? You really do, don't you?'

'Yes!'

'OK, I perfectly understand you.'

The boy was satisfied and did not interrupt again. His urge to be listened to was greater than his urge to go out.

Doug does not tell us how his story ends. However, in cases as this, it is highly recommended to take care of the child as soon as the phone call is over. Otherwise, listening becomes an unethical and short-lived form of manipulation. Listening must continue to be mainly the most natural way of understanding others.

An old saying in ancient Rome was, 'Caesar's wife must not only be honest but also appear to be honest'. The same applies to listening. When listening, one must also appear to be listening. Patrick McWinney, a Canadian theologist who has specialised in mediation, talked to me enthusiastically about this, and gave me some advice I have found quite useful.

31. I Am All Ears

Patrick claims that in order to make a person feel listened to we must put our whole body to the task of listening. This includes our eyes, expressions, nods, exclamations, and body language: to be 'all ears', as the saying goes.

'All that glitters is not gold,' states a popular saying, although I do not think it can be applied to listening. Through personal experience, I find it is very hard to show one is listening unless one really is listening. And, after listening, it is hard not to feel some empathy for the other person and have a greater disposition to co-operate. We often get anxious and impatient when listening to a person because we think we already know what the person is thinking. To help us gain awareness of this, Bob Bordone had a simple exercise.

32. Lying on the Floor

All participants would be asked to write a couple of paragraphs on what we imagined we would feel if we lay down on the floor. Next we were asked to leave our desks and lie down right there, on the classroom floor. One minute later he would ask if there were any differences between what we had supposed would happen and what actually had happened. The differences were huge. I recall lying on my back, gazing at the ceiling and discovering dark wooden beams I had not noticed until that moment. Nor had I anticipated the pungent scent left by the carpet cleaning product, nor my classmates' giggling.

'Imagine,' Bob would continue. 'How difficult it is to guess what a person in a different situation, with a different background and personality, would feel, if it is already so difficult to guess what you would feel lying on the floor, barely a couple of feet away.'

Although checking one's assumptions is important because information may contain errors, it is also useful to take into account differences of perception and varying points of view. Patrick McWinney once told me the following:

33. Hot or Cold

'It's hot today. But that is how I feel coming from Canada. For you, who come from Buenos Aires, it's cold. This difference is easy enough to imagine, but there are others which are not as obvious, and they can tangle up a negotiation by making us jump to the wrong assumption.'

A situation can worsen if it is not to the advantage of one of the parties to admit the other party's point of view.

34. Alice

A developer is working to turn an 'ugly looking swamp' into a 'splendid country club', which will create new jobs and raise taxes for communal welfare. She considers these to be sound and logical arguments. She thinks it absurd that insects, frogs and birds that inhabit the swamp may be of fundamental importance for the survival of a broad spectrum of species, and that this be considered an acceptable value. It is so absurd to her, she is not even willing to discuss it. She just cannot understand it. 'How can mosquitoes be more important than people?' she asks ironically. She would perhaps be willing to understand that what is cold weather to her, may be warm weather for a Canadian, as this concept does not affect her business. But she refuses to accept that someone may conclude, after having studied ecology for a lifetime, that swamp areas play a vital role, and its elimination will cut short the life cycle of countless species, interrupt the food chain, interfere with the migration of birds, and end up seriously affecting some human interests.

A discussion can be made up of a series of monologues or a fruitful exchange of information.

35. The Young Priest

A newly ordained priest enthusiastically started to work at the parish he had been assigned to. Every day he toured the neighbourhood preaching God's word to the families in his community. He would walk tirelessly from dawn till dusk, visiting every home to talk about God and the salvation of the soul. When Sunday arrived he would dutifully work on his sermon and wait anxiously for the large gathering that would surely attend. But only a few showed up. Then, somewhat disillusioned but his resolve untainted, he would remind himself that no one had promised him an easy job, and he should double his efforts. He would rise earlier, visit more people and speak more passionately. Still he was unable to achieve results. One day he fell ill and was forced to remain in bed. His deacon stopped by to see him and asked him how he was getting along. Consumed by fever and exhausted as he was, he barely had strength enough to confess his dispirit. The deacon listened in silence. Before leaving, he patted the young priest's back understandingly.

'You mustn't worry, you are a good priest.' he said. 'When you visit your folk, just try talking a little less and listening a little more.'

Still not fully recovered, the young priest went back on his daily visits. He was too weak to talk, and all he could do was listen. He began to discover who his folk were. And the following Sunday he had a full church.

When we realise something is not working well the best thing is to stop. Often listening is the best way to pull out of a deadlocked negotiation. It is important to identify what is obstructing our ability to listen. It usually has more to do with feelings than with other external influences.

On the subject of not letting our feelings interfere with our relationship with others there is a story by Nasrudim which, perhaps because of its gross exaggerations, has proved very useful to me, particularly when working as a mediator. A mediator must be capable of listening to each party without allowing her beliefs or feelings to interfere with the job.

36. Charity

A beggar would always be sitting next to the entrance to the temple Nasrudim attended. On his way out from the weekly service, Nasrudim would give the beggar four coins. Once, because his business was not going well, he gave him only two coins. The beggar looked up in surprise.

'What's this?' he asked irately. 'Why are you giving me two coins when you have always given me four?'

'You see,' Nasrudim explained. 'My business has been poor lately and I am not in a good economic position.'

The beggar frowned. 'Why should I be to blame if your business is poor?' he replied.

People are often somewhat alarmed when I describe the uncontaminated role I expect from myself as a mediator. They ask me where I've left my ideals. Or whether it can be good to listen to and try to understand someone whose proposal is unjust or immoral. I am far from having the final answers to these questions. But we can shed some light and draw nearer to the answer. For example by borrowing the following words from Robert Mnookin.

37. Listening Does Not Mean Agreeing

Robert Mnookin was a Professor of Negotiation at Harvard University's School of Law. When he talked to us about active listening he would more or less say the following:

'As a Jew, I can actively listen to a neo-Nazi as he explains his theories to me, show that I have not missed anything that was said, and that I understand what he feels and believes in. To do this, I do not need to tell him that I agree with or support such ideas.'

Yet if Robert were to argue with this person, after showing that he had listened and understood, he would be in a better position to do so. Satisfying the other person's need to be listened to, and showing that he had understood would have earned him enough moral authority to make his point. And if it were at all possible for this person to change his views by way of debate, Robert would stand a better chance of success by following this course of action. Therefore, rather than setting aside his values and ideals, the good listener is on the way to achieving them faster.

38. The Sun, the Wind and the Hiker

The sun and the wind were arguing over who was the mightier of the two when, in the distance, they spotted a hiker, wrapped in his cape, working his way along a solitary trail.

'Do you doubt my strength?' roared the wind. 'Watch me strip that man of his cape!' And he began blowing a tremendous gale. But the stronger he blew, the tighter the hiker hung on to his cape. The wind was about to blow the man off, cape and all, when the sun asked him to let him try his own method. He gently shone his rays on the hiker who gradually began to relax and feel hot. Soon after he took his cape off.

Power does not lie in doing things, but in creating conditions for others to be able to do them by themselves.

A sign hung on the blacksmith's wall, at the Mounted Grenadiers regiment, where I did part of my military service. It read, 'Letting them learn is better than teaching them.' My son Simon's kindergarten teacher once said to me, 'Children don't learn things they don't ask themselves.' And a popular saying goes, 'The master arrives when the disciple is ready.' Also along this train of thought is Bill Moomaw's advice on being careful not to rush a process.

39. Speed

Bill is a scientist who specialises in the environmental problems caused by human development, particularly those that involve the atmosphere and climatic changes. He was the first scientist to be appointed advisor to the US Congress. He recognises the importance of skillful negotiation to implement solutions that, from a scientific point of view, are obvious, essential and urgent. Together with Larry Susskind he directs a programme for sustainability management through which officials from all over the world are trained in eight-day workshops held in Holland. At these workshops negotiation exercises are carried out. I was an assistant at one of these workshops and took great pleasure in discussing a variety of subjects with Bill, as we jogged on several mornings across the Woodschoten Forest. He taught me the phrase, 'Move slowly in order to advance fast', and he explained that, 'No matter how just your motives or how right you may be, if you push the issue too fast it will be resisted'. Napoleon used to say to the valet who helped him dress, 'Don't rush, I'm in a hurry.'

Nature will sometimes teach us the same lesson.

40. Walking on Ice

In the winter of the year I lived in Cambridge, Massachusetts, some nearby lakes froze over. Coming from the mild winters of Buenos Aires, this was new to me. A friend explained that walking on ice was tricky business, and showed me how to inch forward very cautiously, always ready to retreat at the slightest crack from under my feet. I got the feeling that making headway in a mediation had much in common with walking over a frozen lake.

It could be argued that regarding certain values one must not even attempt negotiation. There are things that are just not negotiable. Larry Susskind claims that matters concerning National Constitution, identity or faith are better left outside the scope of negotiation. And on one of our jogging mornings Bill Moomaw touched upon the risk of becoming too political.

41. Political Gravity

If politicians were to argue over the law of gravity and what the force that attracts objects to Earth was, some claiming it to equal one 'G' and others claiming it to be two 'Gs', it would probably be voted as one and a half.

In other words, not everything is open to negotiation.

A mediator can help parties in conflict improve their dialogue, and do so in honesty, just by being there, without stepping in. There is an interesting story that carries this to an extreme.

42. The African Priest

I am fascinated by the story of a priest who used to mediate in conflicts among the members of an African tribe. What I marvelled at, when I first heard the story, was that this good man's 'method' confirmed my belief that parties can usually reach agreements given the opportunity and stimulation.

The priest would stand in his church before two conflicting persons, and ask one of them to explain what had happened. The priest would listen attentively and then he would raise his eyes and his hands and would ask for God's help in solving the conflict. Then he would ask the other person to explain his or her view of the disagreement. And once again he would hear out the story and make a new request for help. This would go on time and again, and the parties would end up solving their own problems.

A colleague who once told this story stirred up a variety of reactions from the audience, some cheerful, some ironical.

One person suggested the method was so dull that, unless the parties got down to work and found a solution to the conflict, they feared it would lag on beyond bearable limits. Although I find this somewhat exaggerated, it is true that parties get the feeling that no one but themselves can release them from the responsibility of solving the situation they are in.

Another person said churches, priests and religious rites tend to build up a framework of respect, which is why it is harder to walk out of a church leaving behind an unresolved matter than to do so from an ordinary office. Just as it would seem harder to lie or act selfishly standing before an altar than in front of an office desk. I am marvelled at the modest priest, who doesn't go looking for clever arguments to influence either party in conflict, but begs God's help and lets the two parties talk to each other time after time.

A mediator, I believe, is assisted by a certain amount of resignation and the full awareness of his or her limitations. The Tao Te Ching says a wise leader must do very little, and John Hider, in his book titled *The Tao of Leadership,* uses a metaphor I find very appropriate.

43. The Midwife

Hider talks of leaders in terms that befit a mediator. He maintains the leader must assist the group as a midwife would assist during a birth. It is obvious that the main actors in a birth are the mother and the child, and that the child's creators are the parents. The metaphor is particularly appropriate for mediators. The parties will trust the mediator regarding the process, just as the parents will trust the midwife, but they are still responsible for the outcome, just as the parents are for the child.

The idea of a mediator with an inactive role in the conflict is difficult to accept, in contrast with a generally accepted image of the skillful, diplomatic, subtle and perceptive mediator with a sound knowledge of psychology and a balanced spirit. This apparent contradiction deserves some clarification. The words of the Indian Jesuit Anthony De Mello come to mind, 'If you believe doing little is easy, give it a try and you will see all the work it involves.' It is worth pointing out that, however little, the part the mediator plays is important. An old story of a boiler repairman relates to this point.

44. Big Bang

A boiler had not been working properly in a small factory, and no one in the company understood what was wrong with it or how to fix it. It was finally decided to call in a specialist. A repairman arrived and was shown to the boiler room. After studying the case thoughtfully, he opened his toolbox and produced a large hammer with which he pounded the boiler with a tremendous force. From that moment on the boiler worked normally and the man made out a bill for one hundred dollars.

The manager's jaw dropped when he saw the bill.

'Do you mean to say you charge a hundred dollars for one bang with your hammer?'

'No,' said the repairman. 'That's only one dollar, the other ninety nine are for knowing where to hit.'

An absolute must for a mediator is to have complete trust from the parties involved. This is no small achievement. The outcome may be influenced more by things one avoids doing than by what one actually does. The people who called in the boiler repairman trusted him enough to let him do what he ended up doing. The basic element in the mediator's task is trust. With trust a mediator can function. Without it a mediator is stalled. A couple of incidents I witnessed have made me give this matter much thought.

When I discovered a vocation for mediation in me, I was troubled by doubts whether I was really up to it. Out of admiration, I held the role of a mediator so high it seemed beyond reach. I had participated in several workshops and had been emphatically encouraged to pursue a career in mediation, yet I felt it was not up to me to tell others how to solve their problems.

45. The Retiro Traffic Lights

One day, walking along the streets of Buenos Aires, I was awestruck by an incident I witnessed. At a major intersection outside the Retiro train station the traffic lights were out of order. It was during the morning rush hour and thousands of people were headed for their offices. But nobody could move. The intersection was blocked by a gigantic traffic jam, and hundreds of cars and buses struggled fruitlessly to inch forward. An endless stream of vehicles lined up the avenues leading to the intersection while fresh waves of young executives, eager to start a new day's work, tagged on to the frustrating deadlock.

It made a sad sight. I could not help but stare at those well-dressed people behind the wheels of their expensive cars. Most of them were likely to be well-trained professionals. Yet their talents were being hopelessly wasted. Those back in line bore faces of anxiety and frustration. Those in the eye of the traffic jam made futile attempts to push through, although they could see it was impossible for the vehicles ahead of them to get out of their way. Some blew their horns exasperatedly.

There was a crowd of capable people sitting in high technology automobiles completely immobilised. What had gone wrong? Surely not the policy applied by the current administration, nor the chemical formula of the fuel their engines burned. It was no subtle social agreement among political sectors. In fact what had gone wrong was a device that alternately showed red, green and yellow lights. And its greatest merit lay not in the manner in which it beamed its signals but in having got people to transfer authority to it, thus letting themselves be coordinated by it.

I suddenly had a vision of conflicts worldwide being mishandled, as was the case at this chaotic intersection. Probably in a less obvious way, since most conflicts take place away from the public eye behind the Congress walls, in business offices, universities, hospitals, even peace talks or arms control negotiations. I then understood that playing the role of a traffic light is not difficult. But one needs to be awarded that role. A mediator cannot exist without the trust of the parties.

It has taken me quite some time to accept that the essence of the mediator lies in being rather than doing. Yet I can still hear the incessant queries of an impatient inner voice urging, 'Oh! Don't come to me with those dull answers. I want to know what the mediator does to pacify the beasts. Does he hypnotise them? Does he sing to them? What tricks can you teach me? How do you stop a charging bull? Do you use their own strength against them?'

Not that I wouldn't like to play the wise hero, who can magically solve conflicts. Like most people, I have incorporated a Hollywood movie style model, where the good guy defeats evil and everybody is grateful. The youth inside me still hangs on to this ambition. But I have learnt to value a lesser role. In *The Tao of Leadership*, John Hider explains that a leader who shines, blinds. I keep telling myself that the less I do the better.

And the younger me insists, 'Obviously, you must do something, you must have one objective. Don't play hard to get and tell me.'

That much is true. I do have a general framework. I start off from the principle that, in a conflict, there may be opposed positions but it will be difficult to come across opposed interests. We have seen this in the stories of the orange and the German trainee. Both girls claimed the same orange. Their positions were one hundred percent opposed, yet one wanted the pulp and the other the skin. Their interests were not at all opposed. But dialogue and forthrightness are the first casualties in a conflict. Let us imagine the following situation.

46. Unlikely Dialogue (The Orange Revisited)

The argument over the orange has escalated and the girls have become belligerent. They are pulling each other's hair; sticking their fingers in each other's eyes and biting one another.

'What do you want the orange for?' one of them asks sweetly without letting go the leg trapped between her jaws.

'I want to cook some marmalade, and you?'

'I'd like to eat the pulp.'

'Well, that's a stroke of luck because, to cook marmalade, all I need is the skin.'

'Let's stop this fight right now then, since we'll each get what we want regardless of what the other gets.'

Of course this is unlikely to happen. What makes it unlikely is that fighting and dialogising are incompatible. Certain basic conditions required to have a dialogue are lost in confrontation. As a consequence of this, it does not seem convenient to supply the enemy with information. Tension closes the mind and frightens off imagination. Fighting has short time spells while teamwork requires patience.

Passing from positions to interests, and then on to options is a highly effective conflict-solving method. One wonders why conflicts exist at all, when such simple solutions lie at hand. Why won't the two girls quarrelling over the orange spontaneously turn to discuss their interests? Why hasn't this been naturally absorbed by our culture, and why don't all humans use it as they use a language or a smile? In fact I believe it is used most of the time, and that is why conflicts tend to be an exception in human relationships.

Yet certain circumstances interfere with open dialogue and divert energy from co-operation to combat. Once this happens we begin to see the other as the evil character in the plot. At this point it becomes very hard to return to a co-operation situation. While the girls are sticking their fingers in each other's eyes and pulling each other's hair over an orange it would be unthinkable for one to turn to the other and say, 'Just a moment, what is it you want the orange for?' in an attempt to steer away from positions and draw nearer to interests.

And even if this unlikely question were asked, the most probable reply would be, 'To shove it into your ear, you fool!' since the atmosphere of conflict does not offer the girls sufficient guarantee to trust each other and share their true plans and feelings.

47. Housing a Dialogue

Restoring conditions that favour dialogue is the mediator's first objective. As a memory aid I use a very simple model, which combines three important principles that are often left out in the rush of a conflict. The model I use is a house, which is a symbol for security and comfort.

I first draw the roof, which stands for the need to have a physical location to hold a dialogue. For it to be adequate, this location must be on neutral ground, since parties in conflict are usually extremely sensitive to bias, whether real or false. It is important to avoid interruptions of any sort, and to prevent people who are not connected with the negotiation from wandering by. Care should be taken so that the proceedings are not seen or overheard by others. The space should be comfortably designed, well ventilated and illuminated, and equipped with the necessary support technology. It is also important to show respect for participants, as their self-esteem may be going through a crisis. The physical location is the symbol and proof that the negotiation is in good hands and that things will turn out well. If the location is adequate it will inspire trust and support for the process.

I then proceed to draw the walls of the house, a symbol for psychological containment. In practice, they represent those who bring the parties together, the mediators or facilitators and the rules of the game agreed upon at the start of the process. These rules guarantee no one will come away offended, that customs will be observed, and that nothing will be decided unless all participants are in absolute agreement. Facilitators are often the visible side of a broader organisation which includes the conveners. The conveners are those who call in the parties to negotiate. They should be persons of prestige, a high moral standing and, above all, unquestioned impartiality. Their role is one of insurance. They stimulate trust, and encourage adhesion to the dialogue process.

Finally I draw a horizontal arrow at the house's ground level, as a symbol for time. The parties must be committed to participate in the negotiation process for a minimum period of time. If the duration of this period is not pre-established, facilitators are unable to plan their activities. Furthermore, at the first sign of tension, either party might consider it legitimate to withdraw and drop the negotiation. As often happens in personal relationships, a heated argument may serve to uncover things which had piled up, and which would not have been aired were it not for the stimulus provided by the fight. Drawing such things out and discussing them is often a necessary step to achieve a period of harmony.

This model can be applied in cases where the magnitude of the issue at stake and the resources assigned to the resolution of the conflict command top professional work with adequate infrastructure. However, it can also prove a useful checklist to find out what can be going wrong even in a small family quarrel.

'OK OK,' the inner younger me I cannot rid myself of insists. 'Let's assume you've managed to bring everybody together at this nice meeting room, with a pre-established period of time and an agreement on the rules of the game. What do you tell them? What do you try to accomplish?'

To answer this, I would turn to a metaphor I learnt from Patrick McWinney.

48. The Logs from Canada

Patrick, who is a Canadian, tells us that, back in his country, the lumber industry uses rivers to transport huge logs from the forest to the lumberyard. With the aid of powerful chainsaws, lumberjacks fell colossal trees and log them. They then slide them into the river and the logs majestically drift downstream. Yet, in this system there are some workers who do not operate chainsaws nor produce any logs. They perform a lesser yet important task. They work their way down the river shorelines pushing beached logs back into the mainstream. A gentle push gets the logs back on their journey. Very much like a mediator's job.

'A minor task, doing very little, never shining.' One might say I project such a dismal conception of the mediator's role that no one with the slightest inkling of ambition would ever want to take the job. And yet there are mediators who take an active stand. Larry Susskind supports the model of an active mediator, but I think he knows extremely well when to step in and when not to. Anyway, it is also true, generally speaking, that personal ambition and the desire to act, glow and sparkle, unless steered in the right direction, may interfere with the mediator's work and lessen its quality. In other words, one can bring together a lot of intelligence, skill and ambition to make things turn out in such a way that parties can communicate between themselves, barely noticing the mediator's presence. It may seem odd that one should aim to excel by going unnoticed, but it is an acquired taste. The story of the pianist blends in well at this point.

49. The Pianist

A great pianist was being interviewed by the press.

'People marvel at the way you play. Your style has enraptured the public to the point of delirium, and yet you play the same musical pieces other great pianists play. How do you achieve this?'

The question seemed to intrigue the artist as well.

'It's true,' he said vaguely. 'I play the same notes... play them in the same order...'

Suddenly his face lit up as if he'd just seen the love of his life again.

'But the silences... Ah! The silences!'

To add to this poetic and metaphoric conception let us look at a real life case where things may be less obvious, but a trained eye can recognise virtue in silence, and trouble in over-participating. Kathleen Valley, who teaches social psychology at the Harvard School of Business, shared with me an experience she suffered through in a negotiation where one of the parties was left with no room for manoeuvre.

50. Biased Mediator

A community mediation centre dealt with cases of minors who had caused damage to private property. The objective was to give the youths an opportunity to meet their victims and become aware of the consequences of their transgressions, by letting them see the distress they had caused. The youths were expected to reflect on their past actions, and the victims would draw moral satisfaction from a dialogue in which some degree of apology would be offered.

Kathleen Valley remembers a case that ended in failure in which she was one of two mediators. The case involved three boys who had damaged a car by setting off fireworks underneath it. During preparation, they had agreed that the other mediator would conduct the process while Kathleen would take a more passive role, observing and supporting.

Those present in the meeting room at the start of the process were the two mediators, the couple who owned the car, and the three boys who had caused the damage. The leading mediator felt that the couple, who were elderly people, were in a weaker position than the boys, who were young and rash. Consequently, from the start, she was severe and recriminating towards the boys and showed a containing attitude towards the couple. As a result the boys closed up, took on a defensive attitude, and were unable to hold any sort of heartfelt dialogue, let alone admit they had done harm or apologise for it. The scene ended up resembling a reprimand rather than a dialogue.

This case happened quite some time back, and perhaps the outlook on such matters has changed considerably since. For instance, it comes across as odd to talk about mediation when there are prior intentions to teach the culprits a lesson. It sounds like reforming rather than mediating. And one gets the feeling Kathleen had intentions to treat the parties as equals and allow a free dialogue, a view which was not entirely shared by her team mate.

This brings me back to what it is we are trying to achieve in mediation. The objective is to make it possible for the parties to be able to talk. They should lose fear and feel safe and calm. Under these conditions they can identify what they really want, discover that they could make the cake bigger before they share it, and work as a team to achieve this. For this they must clearly see the convenience of working together. They must realise that they have more things in common than they think, and that those things in which they are different can also be useful to arrive at good solutions.

A great example of this was the Taura syndrome, in Ecuador.

51. The Taura Syndrome

Two of the most important economic resources of Ecuador are bananas and shrimp. Their combined product makes up about a third of the country's GDP (gross domestic product). At one point in time the shrimp production areas were affected by a pathology the cause of which was attributed to chemicals used in banana production. Accusations were made and a large-scale conflict ensued.

My friend Yolanda Kakabadse, from the Futuro Latinoamericano Foundation, organised a meeting where well-respected representatives of both sectors were invited to facilitate the search for consensus solutions. Up to that moment, both groups had exchanged a flurry of aggressions through the press, public administration, court, and social connections. It was feared that the level aggression reached would generate extreme violence. Yolanda had spent some time in preparation to participate in this type of conflict. I was part of a group of facilitators who had been trained by her and that remained in contact with her as associate mediators. She felt it would be convenient to hire a foreign person for this conflict that had Ecuadorians so deeply estranged, and she called in Enrique Olivera, a former Mayor of Buenos Aires, one of her Argentine associate mediators.

When the meeting finally got off to a start and the presentations were made, participants were asked to draw up a list of all the common interests the two sectors shared. As one can imagine, besides patriotism and communal welfare, two major exporters of natural resources shared a number of interests referring to ports, legislation, duties, labour, value added tax, technology, subsidies, financing, etc. Next to this impressive list, the issue that divided them seemed to have become somewhat smaller. The enemy had turned into a partner with whom it was necessary to go over a few problems. It had not taken a judge or a messiah to order them to change their minds. They had done it themselves.

It was their own achievement, at the right place, with a consensus for the rules of the game that guaranteed a safe debate, the necessary time, and a light touch here and there by a facilitator to whom they conveyed authority. The organisation had laid the groundwork, and correctly selected the participants.

Selection of participants may be a key aspect in certain types of conflicts. When only two persons are involved there is no doubt the conflict is between them. However, there are cases (for example those in which natural resources are affected) where there are many sectors involved, and they are not clearly identifiable. Let us imagine a case.

52. The Lake

An industry pollutes a lake. A neighbouring fishing club complains. As the industry continues to pollute the lake the fishing club goes to the press and then to the municipal government. The industry declares the situation is not as serious as the fishermen claim, and that they are not the only industry operating in the area. They cannot modify their process.

Apparently the conflict can be solved among them. The industry could offer the club new and better premises on a nearby lake and keep the present club premises to use for the plant director and his family's lodging, since they have been needing to move him out of the plant to allow for an expansion of the administrative offices. Everybody is happy.

They have gone from positions to interests; the fishermen wanted to fish and the industry wanted to work. They will both continue to pursue their objectives in better conditions than before.

According to what we have seen so far, it would seem like a good solution. Both sides won. But perhaps other people ought to have been present at this negotiation. Being there or not being there, or being a part of something, becomes essential in human relations. It is the issue of belonging and participating. Consciously or unconsciously we are aware of it. Traditional wisdom offers us a jewel on this issue in one of the oldest children's tales.

53. Sleeping Beauty

When Sleeping Beauty was born her parents King Stefan and the Queen were overjoyed and organised a party in all splendour for her baptism. They invited all the fairies, who were delighted to attend since the beauty of the child was unparalleled and she would surely marry a prince. There was one fairy, called Maleficent, the parents forgot to invite. This oversight, which could have been averted with a few minutes' dedication, brought dire consequences upon the child. Fairy Maleficent took great offence and, seized by rage, willed a curse on the child. Before the sun set on the girl's sixteenth birthday she would prick her finger on the spindle of a spinning wheel and die. Maleficent was powerful, but the good fairies had power of their own. The girl would not die, they promised the King, but would fall into a profound sleep from which she would only be awakened by a kiss of true love.

The King had all the spinning wheels in the kingdom burned. As further precaution, the baby girl was sent away to be raised in a cottage deep in the woods, under a false identity. Despite all their efforts, the young girl, driven by curiosity, eventually came upon a spinning wheel, pricked her finger on its spindle, and fell into a deep and lasting sleep.

Till one day a prince discovers her and, fascinated by her beauty, kisses her. The kiss wakes her up and they are married many, many years after the accident with the spinning wheel. In other words, the natural unfolding of the process is tremendously delayed, on account of resentment by someone who was interested but did not participate in the initial conversations.

Is it only a question of resentment? Are we so fussy and vicious we will try to sabotage any decision made without our participation? Maybe not all of us, maybe not every time, but in many cases yes. Besides, there are other very valid reasons to handle the participants' list with care. One of these reasons I learned when I was not yet eighteen, and Argentina had a de facto military government.

54. The Garbage Compactor

For years in the city of Buenos Aires incinerators were used to burn household garbage. Each apartment building had one installed somewhere in the basement and the garbage from every apartment was burned in them every morning. In a city of several million people, this caused a thick dark grey cloud that blocked out the sky. Soot and ash used to be part of everyday life. I have a memory of blackened shirt collars at the end of the day. One day the government issued a bylaw whereby all building owners had to replace their incinerators with compactors. The purpose of the compactors was to pack garbage so that it would take up less room, thus reducing the number of trucks required to haul garbage to the city dumps.

It did not seem a bad idea to me since the pollution caused by incinerators was truly scandalous. One afternoon, while chatting with our condominium superintendent, I asked him how he was getting on with the compactor that had been installed in the basement.

'I don't use it,' he answered dryly. 'Nobody consulted me before buying it.'

I stared at him in puzzlement. He was a dim-witted man whose long curving nose hung down almost hiding his mouth, and he resembled a comic-strip character known for his clumsiness. He was also the only grown-up person who could not read or write whom I had known up to that moment. The thought of the Military Junta in consultation with my building's superintendent amused my irreverent teenage mind and I smiled scornfully. It was then that I made a sarcastic remark I am still purging to this day.

'I can't believe they didn't summon you to give your opinion before enacting legislation.'

'Nobody said nothin,' he retorted, his voice showing suppressed anger, and he then added something that wiped the smirk off my face. 'That machine packs 50 kilo bags, and it's downstairs in the basement. The first day I tried hauling one up, not only couldn't I lift it, but for a whole week I had such a sore back I had trouble walking.'

Some years later I started working with the Fundacion Ambiente y Recursos Naturales (Environment and Natural Resources Foundation) whose mission was, 'to improve the quality of decisions made regarding the environment'. Pedro Tarak, its executive director, once told me that participation of all those involved was one way to ensure that decisions were made based on as much information as possible. This brought back fond memories of the superintendent and the lesson in modesty he had taught me.

It was around that time that the concept of 'total quality' caught on. One of the principles of total quality is that a person performing a certain task is in the best position to offer an opinion on how to improve that task. This idea caused quite a shake-up and, at some companies, the organisation chart was turned upside down. A revolutionary concept was introduced: management is at the service of those who deal with the public. The president of Scandinavian Airlines, for example, one day phoned a pilot whose flight departure had had a half-hour delay and asked how he could help him prevent this from happening again.

What was revolutionary about this was that authority began to be recognised in lower-ranking employees on account of the information they handled. Employees that worked in contact with the public started getting invited to meetings and being listened to, not just told what to do. And people from different sections of companies were brought together to participate in planning meetings and brainstorms. Imagine the chaos at those first meetings. Or the difficulties that may arise when all those involved in the case of the polluted lake are brought to a meeting and put into the same room: the natives, whose ancestors have lived on the lakeshores for centuries, the industry accused of polluting, other industries also responsible for pollution, the government who would like to protect the lake but is responsible for discharging sewage water with inadequate treatment, fishermen, environmental organisations, unions who do not want their industry to move away, the chamber of tourism hotels which doesn't want to lose business, the state government and the federal government who have different objectives in their industry and environmental areas. Perhaps it was this chaos that brought about the need for facilitators and all those theories about how to make meetings work better.

Undoubtedly the road to consensus decision processes is laden with obstacles. For each one of them a solution must be found. The first step is to understand what is happening, to identify the problem. Distrust, 'demonisation', reactive devaluation, attachment to a position and lack of communication are some usual problems. Sometimes elements which are part of the traditional system get in the way and hinder the removal of obstacles. For example, let us take a look at a problem of doctors' distrust when one was accused of malpractice in the United States.

55. Malpractice

When a patient feels he or she has been harmed by a doctor, emotions often play an important role. A lawyer once told me, during a conversation about litigation, that clients are usually not too concerned with the fees and costs of a lawsuit because they are more interested in making the other party pay and suffer than in whatever they stand to gain. Although admitting this to be part of our nature may be unpleasant, we should keep in mind it is one of the elements in the game. In most conflicts with doctors we are looking at a person who sought help, trusted a professional, and was caused damage, sometimes irreparable. The situation is often worsened by the doctor's attitude, which is perceived by the patient (or his or her next of kin) as conceited or denying. By definition, repair must be ruled out as a possible solution for irreparable damage. The next best to it are compensation and acceptance. Without acceptance, any scale of compensation will seem insufficient. Those on the side of the damaged patient often seem to behave in an insatiable, irrational, almost bloodthirsty, manner. In other words, until the patient and his or her family are ready to accept and forgive, it is unlikely they can temperately consider and agree upon a just compensation.

In one such case, the family members of a man who had died during a hand operation were doubly infuriated because the doctor had at no time shown the least consideration towards them. He had been absolutely cold and distant. He had announced this shocking and totally unexpected death with a couple of dry phrases and left. From that time on he had never been available to talk to the family, nor had he attended the funeral. His attitude produced great indignation among the family of the deceased. Much of their sorrow found its way of expression in attacking the doctor, in the form of legal action. How could this man not be in the least moved by the tremendous pain he had caused them?

The answer to this apparent mystery is that the doctor was absolutely moved and felt guilty. But he feared his career and property might be lost through misinterpretation of the facts. He knew he was headed for a lawsuit. Anything he did could be interpreted as admission of guilt, and would be used against him in court. Apologising, saying he was just as surprised as they were by what had happened, answering questions, giving information, acting receptively... was all too risky.

Obviously the family sued and had every intention of inflicting as much damage as possible on him. By sheer coincidence, the doctor's defence attorney's secretary happened to be an old schoolmate of the widow. The two friends had a chat and the secretary suggested going through a mediation session before continuing with the lawsuit.

The United States laws (and Argentine laws as well) assign mediation an attribute which is ideal for situations such as this one. Nothing said in a mediation can be used in court in the event of a subsequent lawsuit, nor can the mediators be called in as witnesses.

The widow and the doctor came face to face in the presence of the mediators. The confidentiality agreement was explained to them and rules of the game were agreed. The first one to speak was the widow. She made a brief account of her late husband's good health, his unjustifiable death, and the absolute lack of explanations she had received.

When the doctor's turn came he began very professionally describing the complications he had come across and was in the midst of a technical explanation when he broke down and wept out of control. He made several attempts to pull himself together but the dam that had for so long contained his feelings had cracked, and there was much to empty out. It was a long while before he could calm down. When his breathing was finally back to normal he just glanced at the woman and told her he was very sorry. The widow would not give in so easily. 'Why didn't you say so before?' she asked bitterly. The doctor seemed to have found peace and composure after offloading his accumulated anguish. 'I was afraid you would think I was to blame and destroy me for it,' he replied. 'I was told it was risky to talk to you. It could ruin my career and it wouldn't bring your husband back.'

The woman declined a second mediation session. But she did not carry the lawsuit any further. In an out of court settlement she took compensation which, according to independent opinions, was fair, though considerably less than she had aimed for in court. The intention to punish the doctor had apparently subsided. A curious but symbolic fact is that the doctor's son and the widow's son later played pitcher and catcher in the same junior baseball team.

In a material world, assigning importance to an apology may sound silly. However, words carry more weight than most people think. A phrase by a Spanish opposition congressman, on learning that a government minister had asked for an audience to address the opposition, became famous. He severely warned the members of his block, 'Don't let him speak to us, or he'll convince us'. But not everybody believes words to be so powerful. There is an old oriental tale on this.

56. The Power of Words

A triumphant warrior on his way back from the battlefields proudly wore his unbeaten sword on his waist. Alongside the road, he came upon a group of people who had gathered to listen to a spiritual master. He found a spot amongst some disciples at the back of the crowd and listened for a while. He eventually became irritated by what he took to be pure balderdash and curtly interrupted the lesson.

'The only thing you do is talk! Words aren't worth much. They are swept away by the wind.'

The master glanced at him for a moment. 'Such nonsense could only come from a fool like you, whose cowardly head has been emptied by the blows and punches received,' he calmly replied.

The warrior sprang forward and came face to face with the master, his unsheathed sword ready to cut him down. 'What have you dared say to me?'

'Oh! I had failed to recognise you. Judging by your strength, skill and courage, you must be one of the greatest warriors ever to set foot on these lands. I salute you.'

The soldier lowered his sword, smiled in satisfaction, and returned to his place among the disciples.

The master then glanced at him placidly. 'In the future I hope you will show more respect for words,' he said. 'Words were all I used to make you come to me, take you to hell's fury, and then calm you down and return you to your place.'

From that day on the soldier joined the group that followed the master and was his disciple for many years.

There are times when words are useful, as in the malpractice case, where they were absolutely essential to reach any agreement. But at other times words are not enough. It is hard to leave the trench one has dug in to fight from. We dig in so deep that afterwards no argument will bring us out of it. The motives behind this can be many, and it is up to each one to investigate his or her own. I have found some stories that can illustrate some of these motives. Let us start with the story of the lottery tickets which has no apparent rational cause, and reveals to what extent our decisions are affected by magical thought.

57. Lottery Tickets

The basic idea is that a man walks into an office and sells a number of lottery tickets to the people working there. He lets some of them choose their numbers and others not.

The following day he tries to buy the tickets back. Despite his efforts to keep the prices as low as possible, on average, he ends up paying more than double the original price to the people who did not get a chance to choose their number, and more than three times the original price to those who did choose their numbers. These are rational people who would be willing to admit that nothing they do will alter the result of the lottery. However, the prices they turn down reveal an irrational attachment to their tickets. The single fact those tickets have been in their possession for twenty-four hours makes them more valuable than any other number they could buy.

To come out of the trench we must be at peace with ourselves. Our tendency to portray the other person as meaner than he or she really is, is connected to our own malice. My high-school teacher Ian Seyda once asked us, 'Why do you think extra terrestrials in movies are portrayed as wanting to invade and dominate us?' One of my classmates, Ruben Steinberg, came up with a flash of wisdom I have found useful since: 'Because that is exactly what we would do to them.'

Regarding the Middle East conflict, Leonardo Rabinovich, who is a sociologist and publicist, told me a joke that ties the issue of the accusing hand with humour, thus making self-criticism easier to swallow.

58. Innocence

Two Jewish boys were discussing the conflict with the Arabs.

'What would you do if you came up face to face with an Arab in the desert?'

'I would pull out my automatic rifle and Bang! Bang! Bang! I would shoot him down.'

'And if there were ten of them?'

'I would dive flat on the ground, hurl a grenade at them, and finish off survivors with my machine gun.'

'But if you were walking along, and they saw you first, and attacked you with all their weapons?'

'Why should they attack me if I haven't done anything to them?'

Once you have picked sides it is hard to remain objective.

59. The Brothel

Two Irish Catholic workmen were digging a ditch to replace plumbing a short distance from the entrance to a brothel. The heavy task did not hinder their ability to check the traffic into the brothel. The arrival of a Rabbi elicited a streak of cunning remarks.

'Did you notice who that was, Pat?'

'What else could you expect from people who were unable to recognise Jesus?'

Soon after a Protestant Minister walked in.

'It doesn't surprise me in the least. It's part of Protestant tradition to preach one thing and do another.'

The arrival of an Islamic man of faith was also harshly criticized.

'Even with their harems those sinners won't be satisfied.'

A while later a Catholic Priest approached and, to the workmen's astonishment, walked briskly into the brothel. As they leaned on their shovels, their mouths hanging open, Pat and Michael stared at the door in perplexed silence. After some time Pat said shakily,

'How dreadful, Michael, one of the girls must be dying!'

60. The Accusing Hand

My friend John Nolon, Professor at Pace University, said to me not too long ago, 'Take a close look at the accusing hand, three of its fingers are pointed at the accuser.'

Often the reason we are rigid and unable to forgive others stems from our own inability to pardon ourselves. A great deal of the negotiation effort must be worked inwards.

61. A Lesson from Architecture

When I discussed this with my son Mateo, he pointed out that in the architectural ornamentation of Egyptian ruins, the haute relief, in other words, those carved friezes in which the figures stick outwards, has been worn with age, whereas the bas relief, where the figures are carved into the rock, is better preserved.

To a great extent negotiation implies being aware that things like these happen to us. It is up to us not to let them take over completely. It is not enough to have the intention of doing this is. It requires time and effort. Specialists say the three most important things in negotiation are:

> 1. Preparation 2. Preparation 3. Preparation.

62. Be Prepared

One day two friends got together to play golf. One of them was a great racing car driver and the other earned his living by giving advice on negotiation. They were late arriving at the golf course and the starter was unforgiving. They had lost their turn and the course was full. On the way back the racing car driver aired his frustration: 'What good is it to be a negotiator if you can't get us to play when we are fifteen minutes late?'

The negotiator felt the blow. 'Negotiating is not performing magic,' he said. 'It is about preparing oneself as best as possible to be clear on what one wants, and not waste whatever resources are available to achieve it. Had you driven faster we would not have been late. What good is it to be a racing car driver if it takes you the same forty minutes it takes me to drive?'

'Do you expect me to drive through the city as if I were at the race track, at a speed this car is not prepared for?'

'Well, I see we're getting somewhere. I was as unprepared for this negotiation as you were for driving your racing car along a road where you could not do 280 kilometers per hour. Had we driven at such speed, it would have taken us ten minutes to get here instead of forty. But for that, we should have known earlier that this was going to be necessary, in order to prepare the car and the road. And had we known in anticipation, I could have negotiated with other players to swap tee-off times.'

Preparation, not magic.

Maintaining good relationships with people and enjoying their trust is a bonus in any type of negotiation.

63. Montana and New York Lawyers

During his negotiation workshops for lawyers, Bruce Patton would conduct an exercise in which negotiations were carried out between different people, competing for points. At one stage in the negotiation a Manhattan lawyer made a promise to a lawyer from a small rural town in Montana, who looked more like a cowboy than a man of law. Intent on winning the game, the New Yorker failed to keep his word, thus betraying his colleague but sweeping in a considerable number of points. The cowboy was visibly upset, and during the analysis he publicly called the New York lawyer a liar. The New Yorker smiled in a conciliatory way. He bid the Montana lawyer to reason saying that it was totally unnecessary to act with resentment as it was only a game, and he expected they would continue to be friends so that they could get to know each other better.

'What I know about you is all I need to know. If you'll go back on your word for a bunch of points in a game, what might you not do for money?'

The episode became a classic. We use it to prove that there is more at stake in a negotiation than meets the eye. In a small town, where personal relations are frequent, the value of a good name may be greater than in a cosmopolitan city. The appraisal of certain personality features may vary also in different sectors of society.

64. Same Story, Different Readings

A very important banker was interested in buying a precious stone. The jeweller had a fine jewel sent to the banker's house along with a note, which informed him the price was $5,000. The banker sent back an envelope and a box. Inside the envelope was a cheque for $4,000 and a note. The note asked him to accept $4,000 for the jewel and if so return the box unopened, or otherwise tear up the $4,000 cheque, open the box and keep the jewel. The jeweller, who was an honest man of principle, did not hesitate to tear up the cheque, since the price he had set was $5,000. When he opened the box that supposedly held the jewel, he found a cheque for $5,000.

A young lad was marvelled by this story. 'This banker was a great negotiator!' he said. 'He could have made a thousand dollars without risking a thing.'

His wise grandfather did not agree. 'Not only did he take a risk but he lost too,' he said. 'His word will never be worth the same. In the long run trust is worth more than the thousand dollars he could have made on that ingenious little trick.'

Perhaps the banker cannot see anything wrong in his own behaviour. And many others may agree with him. Others, however, would feel they couldn't trust him any more. Expectations can be altogether different.

65. Joseph's Report Card

Joseph was one of my classmates in high school. Besides being one of eleven brothers, he had certain personality traits that are sometimes considered incompatible. For example he was extremely intelligent but did very poorly at school. A real transgressor, but noble and loyal. He once told me a story that I will try to repeat to the best of my recollection.

His mother did not keep track of all the report cards she had to sign for her numerous children, so he started taking care of his own. He would imitate her signature and save a lot of trouble, skipping the discomfort of having to show his record of unjustified absences and unsatisfactory performance on most subjects. One fine day brought an end to my friend's neat set-up. His younger brother was called to the principal's office for not having returned his own report card with the required parent signature.

'Either bring it in first thing tomorrow morning,' said the principal. 'Or I won't let you into class, and I'll have your parents come in.' Cornered and under pressure, the young brother searched his mind for an answer that would pacify the principal. 'I've got it back in my locker,' he said spontaneously. 'I'll get it for you right away.'

He walked to his locker, fished out the report card from where it lay undisturbed since the day it had been handed out, tucked it under his shirt and, seconds later, was knocking on the door of Joseph's classroom. 'Excuse me sir,' he said as the teacher interrupted his class. 'Could I talk to my brother for a second?'

The teacher nodded and the boy walked up to where Joseph sat and produced the report card. 'Do the signature for me!' he said emphatically.

Joseph did not waste time in lecturing his younger brother and, in the style of a professional forger, proceeded to sign the report card. But as he looked up, he saw the principal peering through the window of the classroom door. By the look on the man's face Joseph was sure he had seen enough to draw unpleasant conclusions. He was not surprised then, the following day, when he was summoned to the principal's office. As he entered the office, he found his mother sitting in front of a table, next to the principal.

This is how Joseph tells the end of the story. 'The Principal kept showing her my report cards, one after the other. 'Is this your signature Madam?' 'No,' she would answer. 'How about this one?' 'No,' she would say again. 'And this one?' 'No.'

That's when I sadly learnt my mother couldn't be trusted."

Getting to know the other party helps to decide how far they can be trusted.

66. The Salesmen

At a subway station, an old salesman in the competitive textile market runs into one of his smartest and toughest competitors, a man he has known since their early days.

'Hi! Al,' he says, staring attentively at him. 'Where are you going?'

'Hi! Joe, how are you?' replies Al, carefully picking his words. 'I'm on my way to Smith's Textile.'

'Look Al, I just happen to know for a fact you're going to Smith's. But you're telling me you're going to Smith's so that I'll think you are really going someplace else. Why are you lying to me?'

'Negociación', the Spanish word for negotiation, is closely related to the word 'negociado', which (especially in Argentina) has the connotation of a corrupt and illegal act. This unworthy connotation of negotiating, in apparent contrast with the heroic act of giving one's life for a cause, is summarised in the famous phrase, 'Our martyrs' blood will not be negotiated'. We have seen how 'the name of the game' influences our behaviour. Following this train of thought, I believe the words 'consensus building' have a better ring to them than 'negotiation'. Perhaps for this same reason, there is a tendency to use the word 'facilitation' in place of 'mediation'. This leads us back to the importance of the power of words. Abram Chayes told me an interesting story to do with names and trust.

67. On the Tight Rope

A particular kind of tension can build up at international meetings. In the case I am about to describe, for example, it was felt undesirable by the majority of the participating countries to have an American in the role of Conference President. This occurred during a process in which the issue of nuclear fuel use and waste disposal was being discussed among countries which owned nuclear power plants. Abram Chayes, who had presided over the latest conference on this issue, happened to be an American. However, since he had done a good job, he was asked to chair the first meeting as acting president. He finished this job and handed in his report when he attended the following meeting. At the start of the second meeting he was again asked to preside, always on a temporary basis. The same thing happened at the third meeting and, time after time, for two years. Until, at the last meeting, as part of the last event before declaring the process closed, he was named permanent president.

Someone present said Chayes walked on a tight rope for two years, which he strung inch by inch as he went along.

The truth remains, when trust is not absolute, it is reassuring to assign power in limited amounts. Chayes held one end of the rope. The other end was held by the rest of the conference members, who were ready to give it a strong jerk if necessary.

68. Ines and Tano's Dog

My sister and her husband had a black labrador named Bock, who became one of my best friends. Tano enjoyed walking him daily. Bock would sniff and snuffle gingerly most of the way except when they approached the front of a nearby house where a large hound lived. Bock appeared to hate this dog beyond all possible explanation. As soon as they came within sight of each other, Bock and his canine colleague would plunge into a fierce contest of growling and barking, their bare jaws thinly held apart by the wire fencing, from which their fangs almost seemed to draw sparks. Snout on snout, the two would bark their way along the fence and barred gate, tearing and biting at the air, until they reached the end of the property. At that point, Bock would regain his composure and resume his carefree trot with an air of unruffled indifference, while the hound remained in his territory.

On a day in which they were engaged in their raging routine they got to the end of the wire fence to find that, alas! The barred gate was wide open and there was nothing to hold them back. Tano felt a sudden surge of adrenaline and had the awesome feeling he was about to witness a carnage he would never forget.

What actually happened was truly unforgettable. As soon as they realised nothing stood between them, the barking stopped. One glanced to the left; the other stared at the ground, slightly to the right. Bock seemed to have discovered an interesting spot on the sidewalk and took a step aside to sniff it. Having done this, they each went separate ways.

It is easier to feign ferocity when there is something separating us from the other side. The popular Argentine phrase, 'Hold me back, or I'll kill him,' blends in a touch of humor into this contradiction of wanting to appear menacing as long as someone else is in charge of preserving law and order. If what is standing between us and the other side is a person, we are burdening this person with a lot of responsibility. And if this person is trying to negotiate, we are making his or her job a lot harder.

69. Middle East

'Negotiating with the Arabs is not the hard part,' an Israeli Prime Minister once said. 'Negotiating with my own people is.'

It is a fact that we often negotiate on behalf of others. We then become the agents, who close a deal and turn to the second table, where there can be many heads with as many different expectations. This conversation we must hold with our own side, to explain what we have negotiated with the adversary, is known as the second table.

Those waiting for us at the second table have no contact with the adversary, are often less ready to settle, and expect a more hawkish attitude from the agent. As a young boy, my father read me a poem by Lord McCauley about an epic episode in ancient Rome, which in time has helped me have a better understanding of what goes on during negotiations.

70. The Bridge

Alarming news arrives about an invading army rapidly approaching Rome. Slumbering Romans are caught unawares. Organising the defence of the city requires time. One of the soldiers picks up his sword and dashes to a bridge that leads into the city. Once there, he stands and waits for the invaders. When they arrive, they can only march three abreast on the bridge, and he faces them. Such is his courage and strength, the enemy is not able to advance, and the attack is sufficiently delayed for Rome to round up its defence and fight the invasion off.

The part of this poem that sticks in my memory is one in which those in the back of the invading troop yell, 'Forward! Forward!' to encourage those ahead to march on the single opponent and destroy him. While those at the front of the line, facing this fierce warrior brandishing his deadly sword, frantically call back, 'Retreat! Retreat!'

This often happens to whoever represents a group in a negotiation. When we make contact with the other party we understand that the issue is not as easy as it seemed when discussed among ourselves, nor is our argumentation so unquestionable. Yet those we represent continue to urge us forward for us to trample over the enemy. When we try to explain what we have learnt on the front line, we are called cowards, good-for-nothings or traitors. I had the opportunity to be present at one such case at the Galapagos, a group of islands whose unique biological diversity has drawn the interest of conservationists worldwide.

71. The Galapagos' Fishermen

The Ministry of the Environment had ruled that the three sectors involved should reach a consensus agreement to outline zones on the islands' surrounding waters, and determine which could be used for fishing, which for tourism, and which zones would be excluded from both activities and preserved under the custody of the Galapagos Natural Park. It was also necessary to reach an agreement on capture quotas and fishing seasons for each species. Fishermen, tourism businessmen and biologists had varying points of view. What caught my attention was how the biologists had gone to great lengths to explain to the fishermen's representatives the risks some of the species were exposed to due to over-fishing. They described the life cycles of these species and their weak spots. They took them on their boats and showed them their research procedures and statistics. With time, communications flowed and became easier, as they shared a wealth of concepts and agreed on some basic premises. But the fishermen who had not gone through this learning phase failed to accept this new vision, and felt they were not being properly represented. So they replaced the representatives and were back at square one. And local hearsay has it this went on time and again.

When negotiating with someone, it is worth keeping in mind that people in that person's second table have a different viewpoint because they have not participated in the negotiation. Everything we do to improve communications will be a plus on the final result. Explaining to the other party that we also have a second table to answer to, asking for their help, and getting them involved can contribute to make the whole process easier.

72. Two Pairs of Skates

My Brazilian friend Rodrigo Alhadeff told me that when he was a young boy his father returned from a business trip with two pairs of skates, one for him and one for his sister. The children had gone to the airport with their mother to greet their father and they anxiously waited, noses flat against the windowpane, as he went through Customs and Immigration. When he had his luggage checked, the Customs officer informed him that he could only bring one pair of skates into the country. Rodrigo's father, a straightforward man who was not used to arguments, stared at the customs man for a moment and then pointed at the glass partition that separated him from his family. 'Very well, there are my two children,' he said. 'You decide which one of them is going to go without skates, and then you tell him or her.'

Each child got a pair.

Being faced with the other party's second table helped the Customs officer understand the situation and saved a lot of words.

73. The Prisoner's Dilemma

The next story is based on the classic dilemma of the prisoner who has been arrested along with an accomplice, both of whom are to be cross-examined in separate rooms. If both prisoners plead not guilty they can probably get off with a very light sentence, but if either one accuses the other, the accuser will go free and the accused will receive a heavy sentence. The problem arises when both of them accuse each other and pay heavily for their crime. Based on this problem, different cases and exercises have been developed.

There was once a little man who lived in a small town in the mountains. He had a considerable amount of emeralds and wanted to trade some in for diamonds. He knew a person who was prepared to make this deal with him. He was the only person who owned diamonds that he knew. For security reasons the trade had to be carried out secretly. They agreed, therefore, to meet one night and exchange closed chests of the merchandise. This would be done through the window of a train in which this person would be travelling past the town. Once the trade had been accomplished, both persons would leave the country in separate ways, and would never see each other again.

Having agreed on this, and while he prepared for the event, some disturbing thoughts began to torment the little man. He was quite satisfied with the deal, but he was tempted with the idea of receiving the diamonds and handing over a chest full of sand.

'I must act logically,' he told himself. 'Or I could make a big mistake'. He tried to appease his excitement and put his thoughts in order. 'Let's consider the odds,' he thought. 'The man with the diamonds could have had the same idea, so his chest is likely to be full of sand. In that case, it would be convenient to give him sand, so that I don't end up paying dearly for something that is worthless. On the other hand, he may hand over a chest full of perfectly good diamonds. In this case it would be right to give him the emeralds as agreed, but undoubtedly I'd be better off if I got the diamonds and gave something worthless in return. In other words, whatever the other man does, I'm better off giving him sand.'

Coincidentally, the other man had also decided to use logic, and arrived at the same conclusion, so he handed over a chest full of sand.

Both left the country, and in some distant place, the little man drew a few conclusions.

'It was logic that saved me from handing over my emeralds and getting nothing in return. But because of logic, I was left without the deal I was interested in. The next time I'll have to use a different logic because, what I got out of this deal, I don't find very logical.'

One of the prisoner's options is not to confess and trust his accomplice will do the same. In fact the best option for both is not confessing but the temptation to accuse the accomplice is supported by the worrisome thought that, while he passes up an opportunity to blame his accomplice, the accomplice might end up putting the blame on him.

74. Self-fulfilled Prophecy

Frank Regan and others conducted a study on the behaviour of students recently admitted to college through a series of negotiation simulations. They were particularly interested in determining whether they conformed to classical economic theory, which upholds man will always rationally seek self-benefit. What the study discovered is that this classical theory is, to a certain extent, a self-fulfilled prophecy since students were more considerate and altruistic before they took the course on introduction to economics, where these principles are taught. Apparently these ideas are not perceived as a point of view, but as a model to follow.

To be able to live in a society, as persons we learn to satisfy other people's expectations. Conscience, shame, guilt, pride and fame are some of the mechanisms through which society encourages individuals to serve in it, which boils down to serving each other. Therefore, besides obtaining what is at stake in a negotiation, we obtain a moral reward for acting in accordance with what we have agreed is acceptable. If, as defined by classical economics, the motivation of economic agents is satisfying their own individual needs, we will probably consider behaving in this manner acceptable, fair and respectable.

Most people see themselves as objective and unbiased individuals. This is easily proved wrong by millions of fans of any sport who invariably complain the referee favours the rival team, while the fans of the rival team say exactly the opposite. When it comes to negotiation, it is worth bearing in mind that our point of view is probably as distorted as the other party's. The team-shirt we wear alters the way we are perceived, and also the way we see the rest. As the next story suggests, it doesn't take long for these distortions to happen.

75. Five Minutes

In a black family the mother arrives home to find that her son has painted himself white, which she considers an outrage. 'Why have you painted yourself white?' she cries desperately.

Even before the child has a chance to answer the mother has started giving him a profuse spanking. A bewildered father walks in on this scandalous scene and asks nervously, 'What's going on? Why are you spanking the boy?'

'Can't you see?' replies the irate mother. 'Your son has painted himself white!'

'What?' yells the father, and overtaken by rage, joins the mother in the act of bodily punishment.

In the midst of this session the boy tries to fence off the blows.

'Oh my!' he sourly mutters. 'I've only been white for five minutes and I already hate blacks!'

I heard this joke from a very agreeable Panamanian black doctor who took part in a negotiation workshop in Costa Rica, and whose name has unfortunately slipped my memory. He also told a bunch of jokes about Argentines, but I obviously didn't find any of them at all funny.

76. Whatever You Say

Some years back, for ethical reasons, Stanford University wanted to get rid of certain shares of South African companies, which were part of the University's investment fund. There were two alternate plans to carry out this decision, and the University decided to submit the question to the students' opinion. The students were asked to choose one of two ways of proceeding with the issue. Half of the participants were told Stanford intended to go with plan 'A' while the other half were told Stanford wanted to follow plan 'B'. The students voted.

In both groups, which had been randomly picked, the preferred plan was the one the university had supposedly not chosen. The overriding criterion to choose a plan was apparently based on the following idea: 'Whatever you say is wrong'.

This previous story and the one coming up are described by Robert Mnookin to illustrate the concept of 'reactive devaluation', which was developed by Lee Ross, of Stanford University.

77. Reactive Devaluation

A number of years ago, Robert Mnookin was the legal representative for a client in a lawsuit which had already lasted a lot longer than necessary without reaching an out of court settlement. The client went to see him at the office one day. 'Bob,' he said. 'I'd like to get this whole thing off my back. If the other party will take $35,000, I'm willing to pay and close the deal so I can move on to other things'.

To which Bob replied 'No problem, I'll call their lawyer first thing tomorrow and propose a settlement based on that figure'.

However, the next day, before Bob had a chance to call, the other party's lawyer called and, after some introductory beating around the bush, said his client would be willing to close the deal at $35,000. Exactly the same amount!

Exercising extreme caution, Bob thanked him very much for the call, said he had duly made a note of the offer, and would pass it on to his client. He hung up and immediately called his client. 'George,' he said.

'You are not going to believe what happened. The other party called before I had a chance to get to them, and they are offering to settle for exactly the same amount you wanted to offer, $35,000.'

There was a long silence at the other end of the line. Bob was waiting to hear expressions of satisfaction, happiness, euphoria... but the silence lingered on. 'It can't be a good deal for us,' the client finally said. 'They must know something we don't!'

I have always found it easier to remember these stories than the actual concept of reactive devaluation, which obviously implies the attitude we have just read about, in which a person devalues an offer as a reaction to the behaviour of the other party.

What the people who wear the other team's shirt do can affect our perception of the situation. But also, the surrounding reality may make us swap team-shirts.

78. The Lone Ranger

In this old story, the Lone Ranger and his inseparable friend Tonto are tirelessly riding across the desert when ahead in the distance they spot a horde of Apache Indians on the warpath. They are brave but not senseless, and they wisely turn around and head back. However, a short ride later they face the same situation. They dash to the left only to find another swarm of Apache Indians shutting off their path. They desperately take the only chance they have left, but the Apaches are there too.

The Lone Ranger reins in his horse, looks gravely at his partner, with whom he has shared a lifetime of adventure. 'Tonto,' he says, visibly shaken by emotion. 'I think we've had it.'

To which Tonto replies, 'What do you mean we, you white man?'

Swapping team-shirts, wearing both, wearing one but living amongst people that wear the other. The issue of belonging or not belonging to a group and its mandates is richly inlaid with possibilities. An old saying goes, 'When in Rome, do as the Romans'. Yet, in *Hamlet*, Shakespeare puts a bit of wise advice in the words of Polonius, "To thine own self be true, and it must follow as the night the day, thou canst not then be false to any man". Both ideas cohabitate in the minds of those who shift their entourage.

Negotiations between different cultures will always give ground to misunderstandings. In a typical atmosphere of conflict, it is highly likely that one party will mean to say one thing, and the other party will interpret another.

79. Two Ways to Look At It

Soviet President Nikita Kruschev visited his US counterpart at a time of tension. After the meeting, as he waved to the press photographers who waited outside, he clasped his hands above his head. The photo made the front page of every newspaper and the American public took it like a kick in the liver. This man was walking out of their president's office as if he had just knocked down a rival boxer. What only a few could discern is that, back in Russia, the gesture of clasped hands is a symbol for friendship and unity.

Misinterpretations often occur among those who feel they belong to the 'other side'. The next example is memorable.

80. Jesuit School

A Jewish man had a thirteen-year-old son whose atrocious behaviour at school caused him a great deal of headaches. The man was a widower, and could hardly cope with his job, running the house, and the boy's misconduct. When the school finally asked him to withdraw his son he could not object. The boy did not last long at the next school either, and was expelled in midterm. There were not that many Jewish schools in town and the time came when the man did not know where to send his son. On hearing his distress, a friend, who was a Jesuit priest and head of a secondary school, offered help.

'Send him to my school,' he suggested.

'A Jesuit school? A Jewish boy? Doesn't sound like an ideal combination.'

'Why not? I'll make sure he feels comfortable.'

The conversation did not go much further that day but, with time, the boy's misdemeanors left the father few options, and he called up his Jesuit friend. The new school term was about to begin, and the desolate father could not find a single school that would take the boy on.

'Don't worry, I will personally be at the gate to greet him and make him feel at home.'

And so it happened. The father walked his son to the school entrance where the Jesuit welcomed the boy and led him inside.

Two months later, when the first report card arrived, the father noticed, in surprise and disbelief, that his son's grades were good and, particularly, his behaviour was excellent. He dared not comment on this, out of fear of breaking some sort of spell. But as the second report card turned out as good as the first one, and months went by without a word of complaint from the school, his curiosity grew until he could no longer hold it back. He tactfully approached the boy.

'How are things Gabriel?'

'OK Dad,' was the unsatisfactory reply.

'How do you like your new school?'

'It's OK.'

Then the father took on a more direct line.

'It's just that I can't understand how you've managed this wonderful change. Not too long ago you were getting kicked out of every school and now you are being congratulated on your behaviour.'

The boy glanced at his father in stupefaction.

'Dad, you mean you don't know?'

'What is it I should know?'

'Dad,' said the boy seriously, inverting roles and acquiring a fatherly pose. 'The day you left me at the school gate, that friend of yours took my hand and led me into their temple,' he went on, as he stared deeply into his father's eyes. 'They have this guy hanging from the wall, nailed to some boards and dripping blood, barbed wire wrapped around his head. I had barely recovered from the sight when your friend leaned towards me, put his hand on my shoulder, and whispered in my ear, 'You'll do fine here. He was Jewish too.'

And I thought to myself, one doesn't mess around in this place.'

People often tend to identify with one side. A French film called *Les uns et les autres* showed how this kind of behaviour can lead to war. It is as if a line were drawn and people were made to stand necessarily on one side or the other. At a Negotiation Course at Harvard University we participated in an exercise which was known as 'Crossing the Line'.

81. Crossing the Line

It was so elementary it took me a while to grasp its full meaning.

> The instructor simply drew a line on the floor and asked those under thirty to step to one side of the line, and those thirty or over to go to the other side. Next those who had said prayers that week and those who hadn't. Then those married and single. Those who had been born in the US. Those who had a sick relative... and so on with a long sorting list which teamed us with some, and then with others. At times we held majority and at others we didn't.

> As a member of Conflict Management Group, Sheila Heen facilitated a meeting between the traditionally opposed Greek and Turkish groups in Cyprus. She used this exercise to show the things these people had in common with the supposedly opposite group. What made the case interesting was that, due to the harsh animosity between the two sides of this old conflict, communication between parties was extremely difficult. There was no spontaneity at all. They were going through this exercise when Sheila thought of asking all those who either had a sick child, or had lost a child, to cross the line. By a rare coincidence two people who crossed the line, a Greek and a Turk, each had a Down's syndrome child. Those who have witnessed the immense dedication required by such children can understand that these two persons may have shared a feeling of identity paramount to the deep-rooted feeling of nationality. During lunch they shared the same table and became friends. Then each of them worked with their own team to bridge differences. They became the beachhead that made untangling the whole group possible.

What had changed? One could say it was not the tense reality they were immersed in, but the image they held of each other. Our behaviour depends on that perception. I will try to illustrate this point with the following tale, which is based on a story by Anthony De Mello.

82. The Monastery

> A Benedictine monastery was going through difficult times. It was as if someone had cast an evil spell on it. Not only was there a total lack of harmony among the brothers, but there were no new vocations. Production at the dairy farm, the vegetable garden and the beehives had noticeably decreased. Even the Abbot, whose faith had helped him overcome countless hardships, was depressed and downhearted. At the peak of his worrisome trance, he began harbouring some uncanny

suspicions. Through neighbours' confessions at the convent, he had come to learn of a sorceress who lived on her own in the country, not far from a nearby village. Because he had emphatically discouraged his brothers from superstitious practices, he now suspected the witch had, in retaliation, willed a curse on the monastery. One part of him urged him to be sensible, but the depressing reality demanded an explanation and culprits. Then, during prayer, he would regain his temperance and would conclude that his spirit was affected by the dire circumstances. Perhaps, he thought, he would be better off paying the old woman a visit to verify her innocence and take her off his mind.

Finally, on a day when six cows were found dead from bloat and the cellarer was so drunk he failed to show up for matins, he made up his mind to go and see her. He asked to have a horse saddled by noon and left without a word of his destination. The journey turned out longer than expected and he arrived at dusk. It was that time of day when light turns reddish and the air is still. As he drew nearer the old woman's hut, only the sound of his horse's hoofs could be heard. For a moment he harboured the thought the woman might not be home and felt relieved. But as he dismounted and turned towards the door he saw her, sitting on a wooden chair. A second chair, a table and a scruffy bed completed the frugal furnishings in the single room hut.

'Hail Mary!' said the monk.

'How can I be of help?' asked the woman through her toothless mouth, her lips disappearing in the surrounding wrinkles.

The monk saluted her respectfully and sat on the chair the woman had offered. He told her where he came from. He told her how hard times had been lately. He talked about lack of faith. He said the brothers were dispirited. He remembered happier times. He even told her about the incident of the six dead cows, scrutinizing her face for a reaction that would belie her guilt. But the old hag remained indifferent. Besides rolling her tongue in her toothless mouth, she scarcely appeared to be listening.

'And yet...' She finally started to speak but again she stopped and remained silent for a long while, absorbed in her monotonous, mechanical chewing. And then, as if she had only paused for half a second, she went on. '...The Messiah is among you.'

Impossible things are more readily believed than improbable things because our reason declares itself incompetent and sets the matter aside for faith to resolve. Had the old woman argued cleverly, the monk would not have believed a word. Yet, in very simple words, she made this unexpected announcement so far removed from the situation he had just depicted, and gave it the shining aura of a superior message. And as proof that he believed it from the beginning, the monk kept on repeating, as he walked to his horse, '...it cannot be true... it cannot be true...'

He thought the night was miraculously beautiful and he arrived back at the monastery without a sign of fatigue. He kept wondering which of his brothers could Jesus have become incarnate in, and how could he have overlooked such holiness. 'But perhaps He's done it the opposite way,' he would say to himself. 'Maybe He's testing us by revealing Himself to us in the body of the cellarer brother, hard-drinking and ill-humoured.'

He gathered everybody in the chapel and broke the good news, as tears rolled down his cheeks. The look in his eyes begged forgiveness for he knew that there was one brother, among those facing him, whom he had undeservingly mistreated. The rest of the brothers felt the same and eyed each other as in greeting. As if they could see through mere appearances and circumstances.

The monastery entered a time of splendour. And never was its honey so sweet or its milk so abundant.

83. The Wizard's Ring

The story goes that King Solomon was into the habit of taking off his ring and glancing at it thoughtfully while he pondered over the conflicts brought up for him to settle. When he died there was much deliberation on whether or not the ring should be pulled off his finger. It was feared its magical power would bring evil upon them. Finally, fear overcome by curiosity, the ring was taken off with dread and expectation. On the inside of the ring a phrase had been engraved. It read, 'This will also pass'.

At times the burden of responsibility for our acts obstructs our view and prevents us from making the right decision. It helps to remember nothing is forever.

84. Trying on Someone Else's Shoes

My Colombian friend Ana María Mendieta tells a story which she was part of, during an introductory meeting to Conciliation in Equality, a programme through which community mediation methods were explained to the public.

In charge of the course was a very prim and proper lady, who had travelled from the big city to that distant mountain village. The list of participants included local government officials, town folk, and natives from the Guaviares tribe.

For the occasion, the natives had journeyed to the village from afar, walking from their own remote lands and villages. Chairs were set around a u-shaped table, which allowed the instructor to lecture from the aisle.

At one point during her speech, the instructor explained that sometimes one needed to try on the other person's shoes to pull a mediation through. Her own brand-new shoes, probably purchased especially for this event, glittered. The natives wore local rope-soled sandals.

One of the natives took off a sandal and pushed it with his foot under the table, towards the centre of the room, where everyone could see it. He was a burly looking man, slightly past middle age. There was some resemblance between the man's look and his sandal: rough, weathered and beaten by life. It was hard to imagine what either of them might have looked like some years back. Time and a close relationship seemed to have transferred part of the man's personality to the sandal, and given it a life of its own. The day was scorching hot and, despite the road dust that coated the sandal, sweat stains from the long walk were still noticeable. One could almost anticipate the pungent smell oozing from the old shoe.

The air hung still. Had the appearance of the sandal been accompanied by an invitation or any sort of verbal introduction, it might have thawed the dramatic chill that seemed to have settled in the room. Had there been a word in Spanish, between those two cultures, that explained why a sandal was being tossed into the centre of the room, the instructor might have had a chance to reply, elucidate... perhaps manipulate. But no word was uttered and the weight of the object dominated the scene.

The woman drew closer hesitantly and, by contrast, the sandal seemed more repulsive as she seemed more immaculate. As if sentenced to a terrible fate, she pulled her delicate foot out of its elegant shoe, and then dared not move further. The sandal owner's scabrous voice freed her from the nightmare. 'No need for you to put it on madam. I just thought I'd prove that some things are easier said than done'.

Sometimes, the only conclusion I can come to after learning theory is that I've done things wrong. Doing things the right way requires going a step further from pure theoretical knowledge. Conversely, there are things we can learn without understanding the theory behind them. There are lessons to be learned even from animals, that obviously don't read theory, as in the following case.

85. The President's Dog

A country's President and an advisor were going over details of a crisis originated by a guerrilla group that had taken hostages, and demanded a series of concessions for their freedom. While they talked, the President's puppy rolled playfully around the office. Every so often the pup would bite at a costly Persian rug that decorated the office, and the President would then toss a biscuit at the dog, for him to stop. However, the President would remain concentrated on the conversation, as he was well aware of the ordeal both the hostages and their families were going through. At one point he turned to his advisor. 'I don't see much point in complicating things. There are innocent people involved. Let's give them what they want and get this over with once and for all'.

The advisor did not seem happy with this. His eyes were posed on the puppy that was again busy in his effort to destroy the expensive rug. The President tossed him another biscuit.

'If you'll allow me a comparison, Sir, that dog has already learnt that, to get what he wants, he needs to tear up your rug. That is the lesson we'll be showing them, and a lot of innocent people will suffer for it'.

Perhaps the President had focused on one part of the problem. It is difficult to fight tenaciously for something, and at the same time keep an open mind that will afford us a bird's eye view of the situation. There are so many things to bear in mind!

Mnookin tells us of the existing tension between empathy and assertiveness. Empathy helps one understand and assertiveness helps one act. Ronald Heifetz, Professor of Leadership at Harvard's School of Government, maintains that one must keep stepping from the balcony to the dance floor and back again in order to do and observe; act as an individual and observe; become a soldier and a strategist. It is too easy to make the mistake of acting strictly on past experience and plunge into a negotiation without an understanding of what the present situation is. Along this line, I like the image used by Michael Wheeler, of Harvard's Business School, at one of his workshops.

86. The Last Battle

'Generals often fall into the trap of fighting their latest battle over again,' says Wheeler, and offers the Maginot defence line as an example. After World War I, the French built a defence line which would have been effective to hold back the type of arms technology which existed in 1914, but turned out to be completely useless in 1939. Fast-moving Nazi tanks and warplanes took over France in less time the French could have imagined in their worst nightmares. The complex line of defence never engaged in combat.

What works for one negotiation will not necessarily work for the next one. It is not a good idea to come to today's negotiation ready to apply the concepts learnt in the hard lesson of yesterday's negotiation. There is a saying that goes, 'If it ain't broke, don't fix it,' but, for some concepts which are in one piece, yet out of context, one had better say, 'If it ain't broke, break it'.

Just as the experience from our latest negotiation bears an influence on our next one, there are other factors that exert an important influence. Negotiators are often reluctant to lay the first offer on the table. Any amount offered, but especially the first one to be mentioned, seems to be of greatest importance. It is true that this uneasiness can be reduced through preparation, by determining precisely what one wants, and having clear objective criteria. But there is no denying that the first number to be mentioned carries more weight. To prove this, here's an interesting story Michael Wheeler told me.

87. Roulette Influence

According to Michael, Professor Amos Tversky used to perform a remarkable experiment with his students. He would ask them to estimate and write down on a sheet of paper the percentage of United Nations countries that were African. Before they got started, he would spin a roulette wheel that held numbers from one to one hundred and, when the wheel ground to a halt, he would copy the result on the board. A while later he would collect the answers estimated by the students.

He repeated this with different groups of students and discovered an interesting trend. When the number he got from the roulette wheel and copied on the board was high, the students' average answer was consistently higher than when the number written on the board was low. The students, of course, knew perfectly well that the number obtained through the roulette wheel could have no rational relation to the figure they were looking for. Moreover, they had rational methods to estimate their answers. One would say, therefore, that the number on the board should not influence the answers. Yet it did.

In a similar way, I believe any number mentioned during a negotiation bears an influence on the parties, even if it is mentioned as an example, and even if it is stressed that the figure is not connected to the negotiation. Spoken words are like anchors, and once they stick in the bottom they are difficult to shift. Remarks such as, "I only mentioned one hundred thousand dollars as an example, I am not saying your house is worth one hundred thousand dollars" will not stop that number from having an influence on the negotiation. Perhaps a suitable answer would be, "Even if it's just an example, let's talk about one hundred and forty thousand dollars, which is what it's worth".

88. Showing Up

Woody Allen once said, 'Ninety percent of success is showing up'.

Because of the tension often built up during negotiations, it is common for a party not to show up for a session. The issue of not showing up, which everybody, from the unfledged greenhorn to the weathered professional, can at times be subject to, can occur at any stage of a process or activities that could lead to some kind of progress. In its broadest form, the "no show" issue includes all those things we know we should do and yet fail to do, for some reason. These are things hard enough to take care of under normal circumstances, let alone when our disposition is affected by conflict. Preparing ourselves is an example of an activity we often fail to show up to. Other examples are not looking for alternatives, failing to attempt to move from positions to interests, getting mad at the other party because they will not listen and deciding, in return, that they do not deserve being listened to. In the face of conflict, for everything we believe in, we will find an excuse that will allow us to get around it.

We will often blame the other party in an attempt to justify our own shortcomings. Although in most of these cases we should concentrate in doing our homework, Michael Moffitt has an interesting exception, a conflict in which he was hired to train "the other party".

89. Training the Adversary

During the nineties, an international development organization had made important donations to an African state, in accordance with a development plan for that country. A written contract clearly spelled out what the donors expected in return, and what commitments the receiving party made. In other words, it specified how the money was to be spent. However, the contract was not honoured. This occurred several times, and the representatives of the donor organization began to lose their patience and put pressure on those responsible. After a period of somewhat disagreeable negotiations, during which little or no progress was made, the donors decided to give the Africans a course in negotiation as a donation. And so Michael set off to train the 'enemy'.

This may come as a surprise to those who tend to believe that training in negotiation is geared to defeat of the opponent, putting our cunning to work to obtain as many benefits as possible at the negotiation table, allowing the opponent nothing. Good negotiators, however, prefer to deal with good negotiators. In fact, the donors in this case realized they would not have become involved in this complex situation had their African partners been better negotiators when the contract was being drawn up, as they would not have agreed to things they were later unwilling or unable to honour.

In the case of the African State, the donation of a negotiation course was admissible due to a very special existing relationship, yet in other cases this may not apply. At times one may feel an urge to give the other party a piece of advice, but this is no easy matter. Certain things are very difficult to put across. Sometimes humour can help.

90. Guns on the Table

The seventies were violent years in Argentina. There were a lot of political crimes that the trade unions were not exempt from. Most union leaders carried a gun.

Enrique Sheinfeld, who was a business consultant and witnessed a number of negotiation processes between industry and unions, told me this story. Each time they got together for a meeting the union leaders would first place their handguns on the table. A difficult custom to swallow, even in those turbulent times. Once, as one of the union leaders performed this ritual, the company manager also pulled out something he had tucked under his belt and, almost mocking the union man's attitude, proceeded to place it on the table. It was a mousetrap. A simple and ordinary two-bit mousetrap. The union leader seemed puzzled.

'What's that?' he asked.

'Well,' said the manager. 'You carry your weapon and I carry my own. That is all I need.'

The message was driven home with humour. Guns were not seen on the table again.

Sometimes the secret lies in looking at things from a different perspective. We call this re-framing. It means finding a different and acceptable way to explain what we are doing.

91. Winner Couple

A couple had frequent and fierce arguments. Both were concerned this could wreck their relationship. They decided to analyse what was going on between them and went over each of their recent quarrels. The conclusion they arrived at was that the issues at stake were not as important a cause for their fighting, as was their combative attitude. They also concluded they were both very competitive people who always wanted to win. After a few seconds of silent meditation one of them found a reason to stop fighting as intently in the future. 'I always want to win, but I also realize I wouldn't want to be married to a loser'. That was perhaps what saved their marriage.

92. The Will

There was a rich elderly lady who attended church in her neighbourhood. Father John, who was in charge of the church, was well aware of her loneliness, and went out of his way to invite her to each and every church event, and often visited her at home. The priest could not help thinking that the good lady would soon pass away. If she left her will to him, he would be able to do wonders in charity to benefit the parish community and the poor. So he took special care to treat the old lady well.

The woman was, in turn, very grateful, and the priest never had any doubts things would turn out the way he had anticipated. However, after the old lady's death it was discovered she had willed everything to a priest from a neighbouring church whom, to add pain to injury, she had met at one of the meetings Father John had invited her to.

Father John was absolutely disheartened and even a little resentful of the other priest. 'How did you manage to have one of my most faithful church members leave her fortune to you instead of me?' one day he dared ask him.

The priest answered pointedly, 'I just asked. She said it seemed sensible, since you had never asked'.

People tend to avoid the main issue because it may sound too obvious, or because they believe certain things are better left to delicate insinuations than to a head-on approach. Forgetting to ask is a classic. It can even be interpreted as lack of interest or indifference.

In some cases asking may not be enough. One needs to search for creative ways of asking. The following story is a good example.

93. Red Canister

Michael Wheeler had worked late that night and was driving home in his car. An important baseball game that might lead the Red Sox into the playoffs was on. Michael wished he had a ticket. As he drove by the stadium he felt a surge of excitement. By chance he came upon an empty parking spot, which he took to be a good omen, so he parked and walked up to the stadium gates with a glimmer of hope. The game was well into the fifth inning and the ticket offices were all closed. He saw an open door and climbed up the steps leading to the press entrance. He crossed several people who were leaving early and one of them gave him their ticket stubs. The stubs would not provide access but proved that there were empty seats. He asked a security guard if he would let him in, offering to pay for a full ticket. The man explained this was against the rules, and rules had to be followed.

Michael's mind struggled to reason in terms of interests. The first thought that came to mind was money, but he could not think of a single transaction that did not imply bribery. This was not only wrong but could also cause the guard to take offence. The consequences of letting somebody in for his own personal gain would outweigh any benefits. What to do? Then suddenly Michael went through an experience similar to Newton's, when he was struck by the famous falling apple. His eyes had come to rest on a red canister on the other side of the fence. A sign on it read, 'The Red Sox support the Jimmy Fund for children's health'. He pulled out a twenty-dollar bill from his wallet. 'If you let me in I'll pitch in twenty dollars for those sick children,' he told the guard. The man glanced at him for a moment and then, with an almost imperceptible nod, murmured, 'Go on in.'

This is the golden bridge concept. Give the other party a way out in case they want to change their mind. At many negotiations we often get on to the right course and find a way in which both parties can benefit. The proposal is fair and reasonable. Yet, for some reason, somebody has a feeling that accepting it will make him or her look like a fool. Be it because this person has earlier been critical of the proposal, or because that person has at some point vowed to watch us bleed. It is of utmost importance to realize that this is going on and, secondly, to create a mechanism that will justify a change of mind. I have witnessed a good negotiator bring blame upon himself in order to close a deal, with more or less the following words: "We would, at this time, like to offer our humble apologies for having supplied you with such incomplete information which broadly justifies your attitude up to now. We regret having caused such a waste of time. Now that this has been cleared up, I hope you will be able to forgive us."

When I was getting to the end of writing this book, Monica Moreira introduced me to Gato Ortega, an uncle of hers close to age seventy. I felt that the stories of his life deserved a very special place.

94. Gato Ortega

They call him Gato (Cat) because back where he comes from in Loja, Ecuador, that is the nickname used for fair-eyed men. In his earlier years Gato had been a handsome youth, a gifted guitar player and singer, whose personality did not fall into place with the stereotype of his military profession. During the time Ecuador and Peru held a border conflict, Gato spent part of his younger days commissioned to a frontier regiment. Perhaps due to professional ties, or maybe because they shared the rough life of these remote military outposts, the men on both sides of the conflict had developed friendship bonds that stood above the border issue.

One day a confusing incident took place. I do not know the details of the incident and would rather not make them up. Shots were fired and soldiers were wounded, and a tremendous tension built up. The incident itself was not too serious. Yet, seen from a distance, from the respective capital cities and from the stately and ceremonial offices of government, it could easily be turned into an issue of honour, patriotism and sovereignty. The conflict could rapidly escalate. If the news broke out the two countries would be on the threshold of an all-out war.

Gato begged his commanding officer to delay reporting the incident to headquarters. He asked for a guitar, a case of whisky, and one night. Somehow he managed to convince his superior and started off across the river in a small boat. From the opposite shore a stern voice ordered him to turn back or they would open fire. Still Gato rowed on. In one merry night of song, whisky, and humour, he persuaded his Peruvian brothers to refrain from reporting the incident. None of the two sides reported it and a great many lives were probably saved.

On another occasion a friend asked Gato to a shower party for a Quito girl who was getting married, by proxy, to a man who lived in the US.

Once at the party Gato was dazed by the beauty of one of the girls. He elbowed his friend. 'See that girl in the red dress,' he whispered. 'That's the girl I'm going to marry.'

'You are not marrying her,' his friend whispered back. 'Because she is getting married tonight. To someone else.'

Gato engaged in conversation with the girl and (God alone knows what he told her) persuaded her to call off the wedding. Although both were thrilled, the girl's mother was definitely not, and she promptly stuck her daughter in a convent. Gato turned to his gift as a singer and in a short time he became a member of the church choir, surrounded by nuns, his fleeting eyes striving to make contact with the love of his heart. Not before long, his cheerful personality had the nuns satisfied that his intentions were good, and they allowed him to pay occasional visits to his loved one, from outside the convent's tall fence.

But it wasn't long either before the anxious mother discovered this plot and pulled her daughter out of the convent. She confined the girl at home and jealously kept guard on her day and night. In desperation, Gato turned to his nun friends who, out of pity, put in a good word for him with the mother. After some time, the mother grudgingly agreed to let him court her daughter, but for one hour a day only. Those visits, strictly timed as in a hospital, were far from enough for Gato. The mother would listen to a soap opera on the radio at six every evening and, as soon as it was over and the clock struck seven, she would sharply have him ushered out of the house. They had not even had time to get started! As soon as he arrived, got on to something, craving for each other, they were pulled apart and condemned to distance.

In desperation, Gato gathered his friends and went out on the streets collecting signatures. It was unfair, they claimed, that workers who left their jobs at six were not home in time to listen to the soap opera. They gathered three thousand signatures, took them to the radio, and succeeded in getting the broadcast shifted to seven o'clock. The mother was surprised her radio show did not start on time, but she never asked him out of the house until it was over. That extra hour finally contributed to their marriage.

Gato and Betty have led a happy married life for forty-some years that would not have come about had Gato not been determined that no negotiation is impossible.

Remembering Gato's example cheers me on every time I am up against a tough case. I seem to hear him say, "Never, ever give up". When you get down to the bottom of things, no technique or theory can substitute will power and imagination.

I am interested in negotiation and mediation because I like people and often suffer when I see them arguing and disagreeing. I sometimes ask myself what can be expected from a negotiation and even, what could one expect at the end of the road from a life dedicated to negotiation and mediation.

95. Power and faith

Negotiating on two fronts can prove quite tricky, and it is safer to learn how through a game than in real life. Larry, who invented the following exercise and has conducted it many times, draws an additional conclusion that can be useful in other aspects of life.

The exercise consists of a simulation in which three organizations which have entered a joint venture send representatives to decide how profits of 121 points will be split among them. Roles are assigned to groups of three participants, and each group is given forty minutes to reach an agreement. In other words, there will be several groups playing the same game simultaneously. Let's call the three organizations 'A', 'B' and 'C', and set the following rules of the game:

> If all three reach an agreement, they are entitled to share the 121 points any way they please. However, if only two of them reach an agreement, the maximum points they can share is as follows:
>
> If 'A' and 'B' leave 'C' out, they can share 118 points between them.
>
> If 'A' and 'C' leave 'B' out, they can share 84 points between them.
>
> If 'B' and 'C' leave 'A' out, they can share 50 points between them.

The amusing part of the game is that each time any two participants are about to come to an agreement in a way that it is fair for both, the third party can raise her offer (at a considerable sacrifice of her own points) so that the other two won't close the deal. In other words, any one participant has the power to block agreements between the other two.

According to Larry, no matter what part of the world the game is played, nor how experienced the players, three types of results are typically reached.

1. The shares are approximately 'A': 60 points, 'B': 40 points and 'C': 20 points.

2. 'A' and 'B' each take around 60 each, and 'C' gets between 0 and 3.

3. In the third type of agreement they each take approximately 40 points each.

It is amazing that there is such a difference in results when they all work on the same set of instructions.

The attitude of participant 'C' is crucial. Results depend heavily on her determination. If 'C' feels powerful, she can achieve a third of the points. If 'C' feels weak, she will end up with practically no points.

Larry draws the following lesson from this: 'If you believe that something is not possible, it will not be. It is enough for you to think you don't have the power for you not to have it. Conversely, only if we trust that we will come to a successful end, we can set ourselves towards it and achieve success through effort.' Another self-fulfilled prophecy.

96. The End of the Road

After a lifelong career in negotiation and mediation with all sorts of different people, a man was having a relaxed chat with a journalist friend. She was in the process of writing an article about him. As was customary, the interview had started off in a somewhat formal style, based on prearranged questions, but had then veered off from the pre-established structure and was running on its own steam. Both seemed very interested in the conversation. They touched on a number of subjects, taking an in-depth approach to professional and personal aspects of his life. Towards the end of the interview there was one more thing she wanted to know.

'Where do you think you'll end up when you die, Heaven, Hell... or in some soulless black hole deprived of any sort of spirit?'

The man meditated for a moment. 'It makes no difference,' he replied. 'I have friends in all three places.'

I have had a fair share of conflicts in my lifetime and have suffered for them. This is perhaps what I least like about conflicts. A phrase I came upon once has given me some comfort. It read, 'I've spoken to a dead man... he said what he misses most is pain'. Maybe it is only from the perspective of those who have already lived that one can realize that pain is the utmost expression of life, both as a mentor and a teacher.

97. "You can't change your pants with both your feet on the ground"

One way of surviving in the desert would be to dig a vegetable garden. However, desert conditions, such as lack of soil fertility, severe drought and extreme temperatures are adverse for plant growth.

A similar thing happens with conflicts. The solution is creativity, yet creativity will not grow amidst a climate of conflict, and if it does, it will be in support of aggression. Many conflicts could be solved if the parties involved combined their capacities to generate value and so had enough to satisfy everyone's interests, instead of arguing over a scarce resource. Paradoxically, in this case, when we begin to refer to a problem as a conflict, it is because certain conditions have already set in, which are opposite from those required for the development of creativity. Those inhibiting conditions are fear, distrust, 'demonisation' of the other party, lack of communication and poor teamwork. In such an environment, creativity will suffer and die like a snail in a salt mine.

Let us look at some examples where creativity can help.

98. Hot water

A European Nation's Ministry of Environment created a subsidy for construction companies willing to use hot water from nuclear plant cooling systems instead of fossil fuel as a source for home heating energy.

Only projects started after the announcement of the subsidy were eligible, in other words, it was not retroactive.

Only a week earlier, a large home builder had announced an important development with home heating systems based on the use of such energy. The project had been widely advertised stressing the issue of respect for the environment.

The builder submitted an application for a subsidy with the Ministry of the Environment. The application was turned down on terms of retroactivity. The parties' positions were, 'Give us the subsidy' on one side, and, 'Subsidy not granted' on the other side. Since it is impossible to grant and not to grant, both at the same time, it all looked very much like a conflict without a solution. The builder was prepared to take the matter to court, which meant a great deal of money and resources would be invested in a process which would not create value but would simply decide which way a certain sum of money moved. Every penny to be gained through a court decision by one side would be lost by the other side, and both sides would lose the resources invested in the lawsuit. The subsidy amounted to twenty-nine million dollars.

At the time I was consulted by a Ministry officer and I asked her about the interests of her branch and about the spirit behind the subsidy. She explained the State was set on reducing exhaust gas emissions which caused the greenhouse effect, producing climatic changes and affecting people's health worldwide. She added the subsidy was intended to begin a process of technological innovation, which would help improve the process as well as reducing its cost, and ultimately be adopted by the industry sector without the need for further incentives.

I asked her what her interest was in not granting the subsidy to this builder. Her answer was that since the builder had decided to go this way before the subsidy, paying them would be a waste of money.

I asked her if it was possible for the company to win the lawsuit and be granted the subsidy, and she replied she thought it difficult, though quite likely.

Having established what the interest of the Ministry was, and knowing that the alternative was a court case of doubtful outcome, we tuned our minds to more creative options. Negotiation offered a good chance to avoid a win-lose situation, or a lose-lose situation, and go for win-win. We brainstormed the problem. The subsidy could be granted if the company agreed to co-operate in an R&D (Research and Development) programme aimed at making the new technology easier to adopt. Thus the cake could be made bigger and the agreement sounder. It could range from trainee programmes for young engineers to become familiar with the process, to expos and conferences where the advantages of the technology could be advertised, as well as many other means of co-operation. The company would receive a subsidy (without the costs, delays and relationship damages implied by taking the issue to court), the right to which was being questioned for having acted one week early. Punishing an innovator for a seven-day bureaucratic technicality certainly did not reflect the Ministry's progressive spirit. The latter reason tipped the scale; they found the solution appealing and moved in that direction.

The question is, why were conversations at such a deadlock, to the point that the parties were ready to take matters to court? The answer is probably linked to our territorial instincts and the reaction those instincts will induce.

When a government official makes a decision that is openly questioned, she will probably feel invaded and her first reaction will be to repel the attack. For this she will probably lean more on personal combat resources than on analytical capabilities. In other words, she considers a range of options aimed at defeating the opponent in conflict. Her angle of vision narrows down to these matters and she disregards the possibility of accepting the 'invasion' and discovering its good side. Her attitude connects to the combative – not the creative – mode. If a third party intervenes, unbiased and unaffected by the conflict, she will not be affected by the same syndrome of territorial instinct, which will enable her to take into account other elements of the game. The unbiased third party must first put an end to aggression, and propose that an agreement be reached on a set of rules to work by. She may ask questions regarding interests. She may call a creative meeting. She will not even require formal preparation as a mediator or a brilliant mind. Her main virtue is that she was not under the impact of what the other party expressed in an aggressive way, and she has therefore not changed to combat mode. She can still see the whole picture.

There is a theatre play by Priestley, *Dangerous Corner,* which is useful to illustrate this point.

99. Dangerous Corner

The first act starts with dinner among friends. The last scene of this act is continued in the second act and it sets off a series of conflicts. It unveils disagreeable situations and scandalous secret relationships among those present. The third act does a rerun of the action from the exact moment when the phrase that triggers off the conflict is uttered, but this time no one picks up the glove: there is a diplomatic response to the said phrase, and the meal concludes in absolute normality. Except that spectators this time are aware of the underlying tension, and can read between the lines and perceive the efforts the characters must go through to live in a disguised reality, which they are unwilling to unveil. Depending on how a dangerous crossroads is approached, results may vary. The fundamental difference lies in the mode adopted by the parties.

In other words, it is not enough to be intelligent and to have the know-how of win-win negotiation because, when one turns into belligerent mode, one momentarily closes off that whole brain section.

This could also be analysed as a question of time. One can't handle two things at the same time. As long as one is fighting over something, one cannot be creating value.

Although we often believe we have unlimited time to make the correct decision on important issues, the truth is most negotiations have a set priority in our lives and the time assigned to them is far from unlimited. The phrase, 'I'd like to be over and done with this problem so I can get on to more important things', usually precedes an agreement which will not give us full satisfaction but will at least end the conflict. We realize that it is taking up a lot of time and that we are not likely to get much more out of it. This is because we are investing time in tugging rather than in creating. It is quite possible that at the beginning of the conflict we made the wrong approach to a dangerous crossroads, which narrowed down our angle of vision.

This does not necessarily imply an aggressive mood. The following story was inspired by a stage of my life when I wanted to give up advertising and work on negotiation full-time.

100. Small Business Merger

A businessman who owned and managed his business was ready to initiate a retreat that would lead to his retirement from his present line of business. He had discovered a new vocation and wanted to work full-time at it, for which he must give up managing his present business as it absorbed most of his time. He talked to a competitor and offered to merge their businesses, letting them take over management. Although both businesses had comparable annual profits, the fact that one party was pulling out, while the other would have control of the merged business, put the latter in a better position to negotiate how to split shares. The difficulty lay in determining what percentage should go to each side. The positions were as follows: the retiring partner wanted a minimum of 35%, and the managing partner no less than 75%. An agreement could not be reached and they decided to call off the merger.

The solution, as is often the case, lay in moving from positions to interests, posing the usual question, "Why do you want that percentage amount, what for?"

Yet nobody thought of these questions. It seems so absolutely obvious that shares mean control and profits, that asking this occurred to no one. After parting in a no doubt frustrating mood, one of them reopened conversations based on these questions.

The answers were as follows:

The retiring partner wanted to ensure sufficient income during the transition years his new business required to consolidate.

The managing partner hoped to put in considerable effort and talent to turn the company into a large business, and was wary of carrying a passive partner whose net worth grew undeservedly.

Once the interests of both had been clearly stated and understood the solution was easy. The retiring partner would have 35% of the profits as long as the annual results remained under a predetermined amount but the percentage would drop once this predetermined amount was exceeded. Both obtained what they wanted and signed an agreement.

Often the key lies in not aiming at the solution itself but a prior step, which implies daring to express one's true interests. We jump to the conclusion that the other party wants the same as we want, and that therefore there is no margin for creativity. It is essential to create an atmosphere of confidence and trust where the parties feel at ease to reveal their true interests, the motivations behind what we say we want.

The prejudice of believing that a percentage share-holding (or even cash) means the same to everybody is a typical mistake which reminds me of the story of a hotel owner.

101. The Understanding Ogre

With the advent of electric light, the stomping by astronauts of the hereto mysterious lunar soil, and the proliferation of Hollywood's special effects' monsters, real ogres fell from grace with people.

One such creature dwelled at the foot of a mountain, deep in some sombre woods, whose name was tantamount to horror and had, in the old days, been used to frighten misbehaved children. In present days those same slopes are cherished by parachute and hang-gliding fans, while the lake by the woods is the realm of water-skiers, kite-skiers and speedboats. It is also here that, not too long ago, a TV commercial was filmed in which young people in athletic condition are seen to laugh without apparent reason while inhaling an addictive toxic smoke which, according to the slogan, transports them to the world of flavour. In wintertime, hundreds of skiers swish down the slopes. At night, a range of trees lit up by thousands of small bulbs conform the words 'good skiing' which can be read from the highway, before crossing the woods.

Faced with this new scenery, the ogre's only option was to adapt to the surrounding circumstances. He was soon eating hamburgers and dressing the way people did. As his new lifestyle required an income, he re-fitted his old house as a hotel. This wasn't a bad idea after all as Pizza Hut and a car rental office had recently become his neighbours. However, the ogre's taste remained horrible, so much so that it turned away would-be clients no sooner had they set foot in the hotel's lobby. Business was bleak. Yet the ogre was a stubborn creature and followed a family tradition of not listening. The only advice he listened to was from a cousin of his, known for her charms. She was a suburban witch who, despite the fact that she belonged to the same family, had managed to adapt to modern times and was, among other things, champion at the local bridge club. She told him point blank that these were times to be more people oriented.

'The magic word is Marketing,' she said. "You have to give them what they want…"

She went on, 'You have to change, the magic word is innovation. You can't offer what everyone else is offering, you need to differentiate. The magic word is differentiation.'

Too many magic words, the ogre told himself as he walked off, his mind set on turning around his business.

Soon after, a sign in front of the hotel building offered guests a new service. They could sleep in a bed that fitted their exact size.

Business picked up temporarily, as a result of the slogan. But the secret soon leaked out. The ogre would personally see that the promise in the slogan was kept. The good old times down at the torture chamber in the basement were back. Short people were made taller on the mechanical stretcher and tall ones were cut down to size so all would fit snugly in their beds.

When we fail to listen to others, and we try to solve negotiations according to our own ideas on what constitutes value, we are behaving like the ogre in the story.

As we have seen, theory tells us others must be listened to, that we must try to be empathetic, to put ourselves in the place of others and so understand them. I remember that when I first ran across these ideas I thought I was being asked too much. I wondered how one could possibly win following these principles. Restless and competitive as I was by nature, I was being asked to become a saint or a patient and well-intended person, like a few people I have been fortunate to meet (but from whom I also used to feel very different). I didn't feel I was ready for re-educational therapy. All I wanted was to learn how to negotiate better. During a training course, which was a requirement to act as a negotiator at the Massachusetts Small Claims' Court, I was taught the concept of active listening. One must not only remain silent in order to listen. One must show that one understands through eye contact, body language, facial expressions, nods of agreement, exclamations, questions and various other tools. I was able to learn how to do this. Even I could become a saint! Through a conscious effort I could now refrain from interrupting, show that I was paying attention, and do all that was necessary to make a person talking to me feel comfortable and trusting.

102. The Aggressive Neighbour

I was reading in my bedroom a few weeks after having acquired this new skill when my eldest son (fourteen at the time) called me to the front door. I jumped without hesitation. Something in his voice conveyed a sense of warning and I felt the instant link between us and completely set aside the complex father-son relationship we had recently been going through as a result of our simultaneous crises, his, teenage, mine, forties. I rushed down, and through the open door, I could see a burly looking man with an unkempt beard who shot menacing glances at my sons (the younger one was thirteen) from the pavement. I stood by my boys and was immediately incorporated as a new target for the man's threats. When I asked if there was any way I could help him the man focused his verbal aggression on me. Visibly irritated he accused my sons of hanging around his truck, and went on to claim they had stolen his toolbox. His eyes were red and his temper vile, which had me releasing large quantities of adrenaline into my bloodstream because, despite the fact that I stood a couple of steps above him, our eyes were level and his arms were as thick as my thighs. Yet I should have realized that something was affecting his behaviour, given his foul mood and the uncanny way he kept repeating himself. However I was too anxious keeping danger at bay to recognise such indicators. After an initial size-up of the opponent, I had instinctively discarded the use of force. Faced with the need of a verbal solution to the conflict, I inevitably surrendered to the recently learnt techniques of active listening. I observed him in total attention and mainly put into practice the technique of repeating. To each fact he stated I would reply, 'I understand,' and confirm by repeating what he had said. I was neither agreeing nor contradicting, but made the man feel that I was making a mental note of what he had to say. Sometimes, my repetitions would somewhat soften his statements. The man appeared like a gigantic tree leaning dangerously towards us, and we were dependant on the power of words to prevent him from crushing us.

After calling us thieves he accused us of being foreigners with supposedly evil intentions, ethnic connotations added profusely.

His temper worsened initially and I harboured some doubts about my method. Besides repeating his lexis, I asked him if he thought it wise to call the police. I did not intend to make this sound like a threat but I did want to remind him that the police existed and that he could eventually be asked to explain his behaviour. Having a police officer within a stone's throw at that moment would certainly have reduced my level of anxiety. Yet the chances of alerting the police without altering the tense balance, sustained by our mutual glances and my constant repeating of his phrases, were slim. Gradually his assailment began to lose steam and, in a final flurry of threats, he was gone.

We notified the police and were later told that the subject was found in an extreme state of intoxication, and very hard to communicate with. In the years that have elapsed since, I have not been able to come up with a single idea that could be more effective than active listening in a situation as the one described.

With time I learned that active listening is very helpful in almost every conversation one may come across. I have also learned that one need not become a saint (I obviously did not profess saintly love for the bearded monster that threatened my sons). One should try to understand the problem one is facing in order to decide the best tool to apply for its solution. A diagnosis is required before we write a prescription. A doctor who will not listen will prescribe the same medicine to all, and only a small fraction of them will be cured.

Yet, it wouldn't be wise to listen to everybody! Good listening requires a lot of energy. Let's take a look at how we can make a small fortune, as listening has a lot to do with this.

103. How to Make a Small Fortune

A well-known Argentine businessman in advertising had set up a restaurant and would give the following advice to whoever cared to listen:

'Want to know how to make a small fortune? Very simple. Invest a large fortune in a good restaurant. A few years later, exhausted by the effort required to manage the restaurant, you decide to sell it. You take the best offer, and you then collect a small fortune.'

The same thing can happen with listening. Listening is a great investment of personal energy. Some people can be especially tiring to listen to. If what is at stake is not valuable to us, we must decide whether it is worth the effort. One must choose the games one plays.

It is useful to have a clear idea of why are we listening, and what are we listening for. In the 'win-win' style we aim at sharing information to understand what value is. This contrasts with the old negotiating style in which individual bargaining is carried out with a minimum exchange of information.

Except for a few very distinguished exceptions, when a person is set on defending a particular position taken, it is useless to try to challenge her arguments since her motivation is not the validity of the arguments but sticking to the position. In other words, the fortress under siege will not be handed over because some of the defending guards are killed.

104. I'd Let You Have It

Children are more transparent than adults and can show behaviour patterns that seem like an X-ray of our more complex strategies. One of the most genial phrases I have come across in my life came from a kindergarten boy. His little friend was asking him for one of his toys and the boy made his answer perfectly clear, 'I'd let you have the toy, but it's mine.'

Next is another example of this childhood transparency we seem to lose gradually with the course of time.

105. I've Been Left on my Own

Several families were spending a few days on holiday together. Among the many children present was Pablo, a four-year-old genius. On that particular day Pablo's mother had left for the morning to run a few errands in town. Pablo obviously missed her and was visibly sad. His grandmother drew near and asked:

'What's wrong, Pablo?"

'I've been left on my own,' he replied gloomily.

His grandmother glanced around. The place was crowded with Pablo's brothers and sister, cousins, uncles, aunts and friends.

'How come, Pablo?' she said. 'Look! here are Florencia, Elisa, Mateo, Simon, Patricio, Carmen, Mariana, Angeles, Vasco…'

'Yes,' concluded Pablo. 'We've all been left on our own.'

As we grow up we acquire the ability to hide the truth and disguise it with logical points of view, and even lies. A typical hard negotiator carries this to an extreme. Many specialists have recommended the use of sly and aggressive techniques. I believe these techniques are used out of fear and ignorance, not slyness and strength. People who are not familiar with creative negotiation to raise value will fear that whatever they say will be used against them. Yet it is said that fear is not foolish. The other party can indeed take advantage of information we have shared with them. Once again we can learn a lesson from Nature.

106. Fear and Porcupines

Fear can be helpful. But when it reaches the point of paralysis, we freeze and cannot move in any direction. Regarding the exchange of information required to be able to work as a team with the other party and raise value, it is important to hand over an equivalent amount of information as one receives. Instead of becoming paralysed, each party should take a step at a time, and learn from porcupines.

A friend asked, 'Do you know how porcupines make love?'

'No,' I said. 'How?'

'Very carefully!'

I should at this point clarify that I enjoyed each of these stories when I first heard them, and those I was part of have no doubt made me a wiser person. I do recognise, however, that a certain amount of enthusiasm is required on behalf of the reader to draw value from each story. Let us take a look at a story that helps understand this.

107. Morning

Paco was a young Argentine musician who studied at a music school in London. He lived with his wife in a small but well located apartment. It was common for friends from Buenos Aires to drop by and stay at their place from time to time. Many of their friends were musicians as well, and some paid for their travels by playing an instrument in tube stations. Although Paco was as Bohemian as his friends, he led an orderly life regimented by a tight study schedule.

Among these visits was one by an old friend known as 'el Mono'. It was el Mono's first trip to Europe and at times Paco and his wife felt it was their responsibility to offer him guidance in the many sights to be seen in London. El Mono did not show a particular interest in sightseeing. He went to bed late and rose after mid-day, his hair and beard in a disarray that indicated he was still not ready for action. Paco gazed at him with an air of fatherly disappointment.

'You must make the most of mornings, Mono; morning's the best part of the day.' Give or take a word, Paco and his wife unsuccessfully repeated this recommendation several times a day, during el Mono's stay. Until one day, for no apparent reason, el Mono was up early. Wearing an old torn and spotted T-shirt, he wandered about the apartment, scratching his head. When he came across Paco he asked in recrimination:

'Is this your famous morning?'

A similar thing happens with negotiations. Even though we may have a stockpile of theory at hand, there is nothing that can replace a shot of personal initiative. And the lessons behind these stories can only be turned into wisdom with a shot of personal effort.

Some people would rather not work on a negotiation. And the best way of doing this is to declare the conflict unsolvable. If the problem is unsolvable, there is a lot of energy to be saved and some benefits to be reaped. In other words, the responsibility and effort that go into solving a conflict can be avoided, as well as all recrimination for not having solved it before.

If the problem proves conclusively unsolvable, the involved parties unable to solve it can save face and self-esteem. This is the reason why it is a common occurrence to have one of the parties talk to the mediator and insist that the other party's personality (or other aspects) block all possible solution. After the mediator's reply, this person is waiting (rather than listening) to take the stand again and resume hostilities with renewed arguments of hopelessness. The conflict they have brought forward is one they have been a part of for some time. An easy way out of the conflict would make them look foolish. That is why people often would rather bang their heads insistently against the wall, than listen to someone who will show them a doorway elsewhere.

We must bear in mind that one's image, one's ego, is a heavy factor in all social systems. If the gravitational weight of that star is not taken into account, all calculations of the orbits of neighbouring celestial bodies will be wrong. Some brilliant consultants fail because they do not find a way to save their clients' dignity, so that they are not put down. One of the required skills in a consultant is working with the client. It is not about bringing in a ready-made solution but about leading the local team towards solutions that belong to them. If everybody takes part in the design of the plan, everybody will have a more positive feeling towards the solution and the consultant. They will therefore not try to sabotage the solution, and will continue to improve it and defend it from future threats. Furthermore, a solution attained by a team is often of a better quality than that thought out by a single person. Consultants, mediators and all persons involved in giving advice are subject to their egos, and appreciate feeling intelligent and useful. They must try to take pride in the achievements of their clients, of teamwork, and not on personal merit.

108. The Trick

There is a technique for breaking horses which is based on understanding their social structures and group behaviour. Horses live in herds, where hierarchy is well-respected. There are gestures of submission, annoyance, and a complex communication which sustains the herd relationship. Some people have studied this behaviour and use the findings to break horses in a gentle, non-brutal manner, devoid of violence, preventing the horse from bucking and kicking when first mounted. Without the typical violence of bronco-busting, untamed horses are turned into docile mounts to the astonishment of those not familiar with the method.

An estancia owner from the Province of Buenos Aires kept a fair number of horses and hired several traditional bronco-busters. He once asked a college classmate of his son, who practised the non-brutal technique, to perform a demonstration at the estancia. The twenty-three-year-old youngster was shy, and his appearance was less than impressive. He was a frail, bespectacled young man who blushed whenever spoken to. As poor as his rapport with people was, it was superb with horses. The local bronco-busters had been forewarned of the outsider's visit, and they may have shown a slight restlessness, although their relationship with the boss was excellent and they felt confidence in their own skills. Perhaps to remove any trace of doubt, one of them stepped forward when the boss was welcoming the newcomer and joined in with words like, 'if there's anything you need, at your service,' beret in hand. Shortly afterwards, while the horses were being steered into their pens, he was invited to sip some tea. But the outsider did not take tea or cigarettes.

The boy went about his job and before sundown there were three tame and gentle horses tied up, and no one had witnessed the sight of a whip or a buck. The ranch hands and bronco-busters sat in silence. The occasion did not reflect the intensity of ordinary rodeo days, and its vivacity had floundered. The boss's son and his friend had to return to college that evening. The father and the bronco-busters saw them off in front of the main house. When the car was gone the boss glanced at the head bronco buster and asked:

'What did you think of it, Flores?'

'It's a trick,' the man replied.

'A trick?' the boss repeated.

'Yes, a trick.'

'What do you mean, trick?' the boss said. 'He's worked three horses marvellously and he's off without a hair raised.'

'Precisely, he didn't do a thing. Where are the broncos he busted?'

'He did three of them.'

'No,' concluded the bronco-buster, as he shook his head and sucked his teeth. 'He tricked them horses too.'

According to popular wisdom, 'The colour of things varies according to the crystal one looks at them through,' and, 'You understand, Alice, as long as it benefits you'. When developing creative relationships it is convenient to take these factors into account. Reality can be interpreted in various ways and people with the same perception can sometimes reach different conclusions.

109. The Refrigerator Motor Started

In the late seventies Blat was an engineer who put together the best stereo sets produced in Argentina. It was largely a handcraft manufacture and production was by request only.

Around that same time there was another character, a very demanding client, who, although slightly less known than Blat, was his exact complement. His notoriety, among the close circle of Hi-Fi fans, rested on being the proud owner of some of the best audio equipment in the world. Blat half-heartedly admitted that the man had never purchased anything from him.

One day this man entered Blat's show room. Blat was notified and personally came up to meet him. The man was interested in an 'expansor' (a device that restores any volume differences sound may lose through recording), but they inevitably engaged in an intense conversation at the end of which Blat was invited home to install the client's expansor and appreciate the complete set.

The man had Blat listen to what in those days was considered superb, a Nakamichi recorder. In the midst of the demonstration the refrigerator motor started. The speakers then uttered some unnatural sounds that were certainly no part of the music. The two men glanced at each other and Blat could feel the air thicken as the suspense mounted. But the man smiled with immense satisfaction and, as he shook his head in admiration, he said:

'Wonderful! Can you believe the sensitivity of this jewel? Just like the princess in the story, who could feel a pea in her bed through a pile of twenty-four mattresses? It can pick up anything!'

A few days later Blat told me:

'We face an enormous prejudice. Had one of my units made that noise instead of one 'Made in Japan', the man's conclusion would have been completely different. Instead of going on about jewels and princesses he would have cursed the national industry claiming it picks up all kinds of garbage it shouldn't pick up, and is constantly making weird noises.'

The group, team, nationality, race or religion we belong to colours our vision. The French film called *Les uns et les autres* portrayed the absurdities of World War II using this concept. We commit a lot of small atrocities due to causes like these.

Each one writes a version of history highlighting events that favour their point of view and allotting an interpretation that suits their interests. If we caused harm, it was well-deserved. The attacks we've been subject to reveal at the source an inborn wickedness which it is necessary to destroy.

In this type of context, with inflamed spirits and boosted nationalisms, the past can always justify hostility in our next move and hamper initial intentions to draw nearer the other side with an attitude of co-operation.

In a climate of fanaticism it is almost impossible to realize one is being dragged into self-deception, at a time one should better keep a cool head. Neutral outsiders often witness painfully how the parties swallow versions of history designed to justify their actions. It is useful to prepare oneself to avoid this kind of bias during peacetime, since once a conflict has blown up, there will be few guidelines. The following two stories will help us laugh at ourselves should we fall into this sort of fallacy.

110. Two Thousand Years

As a man walked down the street he came across another who was busy giving an old man a tremendous beating.

'What are you doing?' he asked as he struggled to separate them. 'Stop, stop! You are going to kill him. Are you crazy?'

'No, certainly not. This man is a Jew!'

'And so what?' the first man asked in disbelief.

'They are the ones who killed Christ!'

'But that happened two thousand years ago!'

'Well, yes... but I just found out...'

I wonder for how many future years the old man will feel justified in taking revenge on Christians. Let us take a look at another case.

111. Ancestors

A Spanish professor was on a South American tour, giving a series of conferences. One of these conferences took place at the main university of a capital city, in a large lecture hall, and was open to the public. After the presentation, a microphone was passed around the audience for those who wanted to ask questions.

After several questions on the subject of the conference, a young woman picked up the microphone and, in a round-about change of subject asked half-resentfully, half-disdainfully:

'What is your opinion of the atrocities committed by your ancestors in the times of the Spanish conquest of America?'

'Well, young lady, they must have been your ancestors because mine remained in Spain.'

We interpret things based on the colour of the crystal we see through, and often our motivation is not obvious. An old story helps understand these cases.

112. The Shipwreck

A young man had decided to travel the world so he took a year off university and embarked as a sailor on a luxury cruise liner.

After sailing for a few months, the liner docked at New York, where the recently elected Miss World boarded. She was on her way to Polynesia, where she would take part in several events and photographic campaigns. Miss World was the most popular person at the time; her face was on every magazine cover and TV programme. Her name was a synonym for beauty. Around the world girls imitated her hairstyle and look.

Shortly before reaching its destination, a storm broke out at night and the ship sank near some paradisiacal isles. In the ensuing moments of confusion, as he tried to help passengers, the man failed to get himself onto one of the lifeboats. He was one of the last persons to dive into the ocean, and as he swam to the nearest lifeboat, he found on it none other than Miss World herself. The storm raged throughout the night and they lost contact with the rest of the boats. At dawn they rowed onto the beaches of a small island bountifully provided with freshwater, fruit, fish, small game, in an extremely pleasant climate.

They soon had all survival problems solved, and being both healthy and young, it wasn't long before they engaged in a most passionate relationship. In the absence of other means of entertainment and lacking inhibition, they tried everything they could think of and enjoyed each other enormously. One day she asked him if he still harboured any erotic fantasy they hadn't tried yet. She was eager to satisfy him. The man nodded thoughtfully and replied, 'I would like you to put on my clothes.'

A mischievous sneer crossed her face and she said, 'And now what?'

'Let's go for a stroll on the beach.'

As they set off he let his arm hang over her shoulder in the friendly manner he would have used with an old friend, and whispered confidentially, 'Pal, you wouldn't believe who I'm shacking up with!'

It is therefore advisable to go a little further than the rational and apparent interests of a person and remember that people are social beings who care about their image. At times, a person's concern regarding what others will say about her is a factor to be used to our advantage. Let's take a look at another case.

113. Late Payment

In a small town a business man had adopted a strategy of delaying payment to all his creditors. His motives remained unknown, but it was impossible to get a single cent out of the man. Those who visited his business intending to collect could be seen leaving in annoyed frustration. The words, 'So and so will not pay' were on everybody's lips.

A travelling salesman who was a friend of mine was the only known person to receive punctual payments from this man. Inventive was his competitive advantage. He faced him one day and said, 'Look, people around here are saying you never pay on time. That's not good for you. It means bad business. You need someone to defend your reputation. Someone who will stand and say things are not the way people are being led to believe. I volunteer to be that person.'

The businessman did not answer. However, he immediately proceeded to cancel the salesman's bill and, from that day on he was never late in his payments to him.

The concept of 'value' lies precisely at the root of the system of ideas that lead to creating value. The first step is understanding the need to create value in order to satisfy both parties. Most conflicts arise from the scarcity of a resource which for some reason acquires value for the parties involved. If value could be created, the conflict would subside. The second step, whose importance is even harder to grasp, is finding out what represents value for the other party. We tend to believe that we already know. Value is that which satisfies a party's needs, or what in negotiation we call the party's interest. In other words, the reasons behind a party wanting what she says she wants. If we learn to listen to the other party we may come closer to understanding, but it isn't always as obvious. Let's take a look at an example.

114. Thirst

A man lived with his grandmother. On a stormy night the man was wakened by his grandmother's voice.

'I am so thirsty,' she complained.

The man turned over in his bed and covered his head with his pillow, but he could still hear her voice.

'I am so thirsty, I am so thirsty,' she went on.

The man realized that unless he pulled himself out of bed and brought her a glass of water he would be unable to continue sleeping. So he got on his feet, found his slippers, and made his way down to the kitchen for water. The grandmother received the glass gratefully, barely wet her lips in the water, and thanked him effusively. Scratching his head in puzzlement, the man returned to bed. As he was about to fall asleep again, he heard his grandmother's voice once more.

'I was so thirsty, I was so thirsty.'

End of story. Yet one can picture the man asking the gods for patience as he sits next to his grandmother and chats with her for a while, until it dawns on him that she was never thirsty but afraid of thunder. This requires a certain degree of sensitivity. Conversely, one can do a lot of talking without realizing that the meaning of the words is interpreted differently by the other party.

Someone said discussion is not meant to bring about a change in the other party's ideas but in one's own. In my own personal experience I have at times become aware of the weakness of my point of view in a debate, but it has taken me several days to accept that I was wrong and to rebuild my theory on the basis of what others pointed out. In other words, I need to go through my own process. I cannot accept what the other party says as true at once. It requires self-persuasion. I am, after all, what you would normally call a pig-headed person. And there may be a great many more people like me. That's why to have gone through the experience is more valuable than receiving advice. It explains why workshops are better tools than lectures to teach negotiation. Those of us who co-ordinate workshops are called facilitators because we make it easier for people to learn from themselves. We create situations from which they can gain experience and we help them draw conclusions. In other words, we help them go through their own process. It would be a lot less effective (and less fun too) if we gave them advice based on our experience. Our advice would be based on our personal experience and expressed in our personal language. It could prove meaningful to others but chances are it will not. It is difficult to be sure we are on the same wavelength. The following story is a good example of this.

115. Frederick

A man went to see a doctor.

'What can I do for you,' asked the doctor.

'My wife sent me,' the man said dryly.

'All right, well, why did she send you?'

'She says I can't say Frederick.'

Raising his eyebrows slightly, the doctor studied him carefully. He said finally: 'Well, it's not a typical everyday appointment, but let's see, I think you actually said it quite well. Would you like to try again?'

'Frederick," the man repeated.

'Sounds perfect to me. Once again please.'

'Frederick.'

'I don't think you need to worry about this, you'll be all right.'

The man returned home where his wife was waiting for him anxiously.

'What did the doctor say?'

'He says I'm fine and I don't need to worry. Now please fetch me a Frederick of beer from the fridge, it's intolerably hot out.'

Communication can be tricky if we're not careful.

116. Marcos, With an 'S'

My sons loved their uncle Marcos who treated them very affectionately. When Mateo, the youngest, was about two years old, he used to mispronounce his uncle name as 'Marcot', substituting the final 's' for 't'.

One day, Marcos, who was amused by Mateo's baby talk, sat across from him and asked:

'Let's see, Mateo, what's my name?'

Mateo was delighted by the undivided attention dispensed him, and eager to please his uncle.

'Marcot!' he answered cheerfully.

'No, Mateo, it's Marcos, my name is Marcos, with an "es".'

'Yet,' said Mateo joyfully. 'Marcot with an "et".'

Granted, Mateo was only two. It is always highly convenient to have information about the communication sender, to make decoding easier. Information like the part she plays, her profession, her personality, can have key value when deciphering. The following saying, perhaps somewhat old-fashioned in some respects, is a clear example of this.

117. The Lady and the Diplomat

When a diplomat says yes, it means maybe, when he says maybe, it means no, and when he says no, he is not a diplomat. When a lady says no, it means maybe, when she says maybe, it means yes, and when she says yes, she is no lady.

Assessing the communication sender with an open mind is part of the process to establish what is value. Open-mindedness is required because prejudice is all around us, as we can see in phrases like, 'A typical square minded engineer' or, 'All a lawyer can think of is litigation'. These oversimplified conceptions don't help. As a boy I used to believe that all soldiers were brave, all priests were believers, all doctors were healthy, and all judges were just. I believed that the greater the importance of a decision to be made, the lesser the risk that the decision be wrongly made, as the brightest people would be in charge and give it their full attention. However, experience indicates that silly mistakes in important negotiations are more frequent than one is led to believe. Woody Allen said 90% of success is showing up, and Napoleon insisted that, during war, a pair of boots is worth more than a rifle. We must get used to the idea that negotiation does not depend on a continuous mastermind, and that many a great loss in negotiation is caused by stupid mistakes made while people are trying to do brilliant things.

118. The Speech

I am not at liberty to disclose either name or source in this case, which took place during the Malvinas-Falklands war. A high-ranking Argentine government official sat at the negotiating table in the United States, during the early stages of the war. In the hasty preparation for the meeting, he had not had time to go over his speech, written for him in Buenos Aires. As he began reading he became aware that the tone was aggressive and intolerant, far from what he needed to communicate at that time and place. Halfway through his performance he put the manuscript down and began to improvise.

But this is not how the event is likely to go down in history. If the meeting is ever reported, historians will probably say his initial hard-line position was part of a strategy, and that once he had the other party where he wanted them, he changed his tone to finally achieve his objective. The Argentine government official will probably not deny this. He will obviously choose to go down in history as a clever rather than clumsy negotiator. And those of us who read this part of history will be influenced by the following prejudice: had the man been so clumsy, he would never have played an important part in history.

At our negotiation workshops, participants often misread or misinterpret while taking part in an exercise. When one team's messenger returns from negotiating with the other team's messenger, she often cannot remember whether the agreed price was $30 or $20, due to all the comings and goings on the subject. If the messenger does not admit this mistake, her whole team will be led to believe that the other team betrayed them. At these simulations, we conduct a subsequent analysis, with all participants present. Mistakes and misunderstandings then surface, but in real life, who would believe shortcomings are due to lack of concentration or unclear communication?

These mistakes are like calculating errors in a maths test. One can understand the problem, correctly lay out the reasoning, but the numerical answer will be wrong. Some professors are willing to overlook these 'small' errors, but real life is merciless. Furthermore, in Psychology, it is considered that these 'small' errors reflect intention, not a minor symptom. This means that 'lacking time' to go over a speech before delivering it is no longer an error. It becomes a telling symptom that something else may be entirely wrong. Anyway, it is interesting to differentiate between problems in the general approach (call it attitude, philosophy, or strategic plan) and implementation (the tactics or actions required to carry the plan out).

The moral in the next old story relates to these things.

119. The Flood

During the great floods that occurred in the Argentine region of Mesopotamia, entire villages covered by the swollen river waters had to be evacuated. A local gaucho lived on the outskirts of one of these villages. A pious and God-fearing man, he was not taken aback when he first saw the water rise on his small farm's fence. 'God will not forget us,' he murmured as he continued his work. The flood crept on, and though his straw-roofed hut was on higher ground, the low end of his farm began to look like the sea with a few treetops emerging through the choppy water. Along this seemingly endless body of water a motorboat appeared. As it drew near the gaucho's farm, the men aboard used a loudspeaker to stress that the whole area was being evacuated, and the gaucho should leave his farm and sail with them to safer grounds. The gaucho didn't know the men on the boat, but he spoke frankly to them. 'In God I trust, and here I will stay,' he said.

The next day the flood reached the house. The gaucho piled up his few belongings on a table. Barefoot and with his pants rolled half-way up his calves, he waded up and down, gazing at the horizon and praying. That evening another motorboat stopped by, loaded with evacuees who insisted on making room for him and taking him away, but he was not to be persuaded. 'I have faith in God,' he said. 'He listens to those who pray.'

That night the man had no choice but to climb on the roof, sharing his shrinking shelter with a few chickens and a cat, as there seemed to be no end to the rise of the floodwaters. At dawn a voice on the loudspeaker pulled him out of a daze and urged him to abandon his property. But his faith was unwavering. He simply shook his head and stated, 'In God I trust.'

Throughout the day the water continued to rise, adding pressure to the weakened walls that supported the roof. Finally the roof caved in and was swallowed by the murky waters. Left with no grip, the gaucho was swept by the current, and carried away from this world.

He had led a good life and his soul rose to Heaven. He was definitely in a state when he stopped before St. Peter, irreverent and indignant.

'Where the hell is God?' he cried. 'I demand to speak to him!'

St. Peter tried to calm him down but the man put up such a protest that he ended up waking God up from his afternoon nap.

'What's wrong?' asked God, half asleep, half rattled. 'What's all the fuss about?'

The gaucho recognised God right away, but even His holy presence was not enough to dampen his incensed spirit.

'I trusted you,' he grumbled. 'I trusted you and you let me down!"

God seemed to recall vaguely who the man was and set his eyes on him ponderingly for a moment while he pieced the case together. Then he stared at him with an inquiring look on his face. 'Man,' he said. 'Three motorboats I sent you!'

Having a clear ideology was not enough. Better tactics needed to be developed. On the other hand there are people who pick the wrong approach from the outset and therefore never hit upon the tactics that lead to a win-win relationship. One of the reasons can be our own vision of the parties involved. As a rule, the mere existence of a conflict implies that both sides hold power. Power is a complex factor to measure. But the fact that an argument has erupted indicates that neither party can move on, or is willing to move on without paying attention to the other party. For example, I do not seek the opinion of insects that inhabit my lawn as I walk out and step on them with absolutely no consideration. Those insects lack the means to counter-attack and they wouldn't dream that the intensity of any counter-attack they could rally could alter my behaviour. We are well aware that our fellow human beings are less passive than these insects and, consequently, we do not treat them with the same degree of indifference. We negotiate agreements, we engage in ruthless wars or we seek middle-of-the-road relationships between these extremes. If one of the parties has no moral problem in wiping out the other altogether and keeping whatever was at stake, and manages to accomplish this at an acceptable cost, we might say the strategy applied was effective for that party. Further analysis would be required to establish what the long-term benefit would have been for this party if, instead of wiping out the other, it had reached an agreement. But, for the most part, conflicts do not reach the point in which one side wipes out the other; be it for moral or legal reasons, or simply because the other party will resist being eliminated. In other words, the power of the other party, whether large or small, will remain on the scene. Before continuing with this analysis, I would like at this point to introduce one of Roger Fisher's excellent stories.

120. The Aeroplane

Roger relates that during World War II he served in an Air Force airplane that did meteorological research. These were dull routine flights aboard a noisy four propeller aircraft. During one of these flights, a bored pilot decided to shut off one of the four engines. As a rule, airmen develop a keen sense of hearing, essential for early detection of mechanical failure and danger. The noise reduction caused by one of the four engines going out had the effect of an electric shock on the nerves of the crew. The co-pilot was the only crewmember who was onto the pilot's scheme and understood the situation. Thrilled with the impact his ruse had caused among the rest of the crew, the pilot then proceeded to turn off another engine. The pale faces on the crew members were already remarkable when the pilot went on to kill a third engine, enjoying an inward laugh. Before they could recover from panic, he switched the last engine off, and they floated in the relative silence of a motor-less glide. The altimeter begun an anticlockwise spin. Sweat beads covered the faces of the crew, as they tried to keep calm and figure out what on earth was happening. When the pilot thought they had had enough, he pushed the starter on the first engine. Nothing happened. He tried the others but got the same negative result and blood began to drain from his cheeks. He then recalled that an engine requires energy from another running engine to be able to start. All four engines were off. The co-pilot had reached the same conclusion as he watched the pilot's futile attempts. He stared at the pilot with a blank look on his face and said:

'Now **you** have a problem!'

The emphasis on the word 'you' is the key to this story.

Undoubtedly, everyone on that aircraft shared a common destiny and the fate of one was tied to the fate of the rest. More than a problem of justice and guilt, it was a question of interests. They all wanted the aeroplane to reach its destination safely. Awareness that 'we're all in it together' is a basic necessity for win-win negotiations. It is what will allow us to stand on the same side and combine our powers instead of confronting them. As an epilogue, and to relieve some of the suspense, Fisher narrates that a sergeant produced a hand operated motor from the back of the plane with which they were able to generate the necessary energy to start the other engines. This is how Fisher could tell the story.

Another wrong approach can be tagging on to the relationship a problem which is actually internal and personal.

121. The Cell Gate

Many years ago there lived a king whose powerful personality and strong leadership had enabled him to push the corners of his kingdom farther than anyone had ever dreamed. His armies grew greater and mightier, and they patrolled the king's vast territory maintaining order and keeping a vigilant eye on the boundaries, so that everything was under full control. He had an efficient tax collecting organization and the economy went well in most years. Religion was also under control. Aside from the inevitable superstitious belief of the ignorant classes, most of his subjects adhered to the dictates of his prelates.

Every so often the king would take care of his people's judicial matters. This was not necessary, but he did it out of tradition and to inspire respect. He sat on his throne and listened to the accusations and the defence, and would finally impose his sentence. On certain religious festivities he would grant a general pardon to all those on trial that day.

It was at one of these special dates that the king's attention was drawn by an accused man who did not join the rest in pleading for mercy, kneeling down and kissing the ground before him like the others.

'What is he accused of?' he asked his aide.

'Sire, he apparently shows no fear of Hell, nor is he interested in the salvation of the soul.'

'Has he been fined?'

'Yes, but he doesn't seem to care.'

'Is he a madman?'

'Only in those two issues, as far as we know.'

'All right, announce that I will show mercy to all those who plead so.'

The aide did as the king ordered, but the man did not change his attitude.

The king stared at the man calmly while his hand reached for the nearest guard's sword.

He stepped up to the man and raised the sword with both hands as if he were about to execute him on the spot. It was a heavy sword, which could split a person down the middle in one swath. But the man did not budge. Gently, the king brought the sword down to one side, a glint of satisfaction in his eyes, as he glanced at his aide.

'An interesting case,' he said with composed enthusiasm. 'He certainly lacks the expression of a madman.' He kept his eyes on the man while he continued to address the aide. 'He would make a great general in the southern frontier, where witchcraft, intrigues and poisoned arrows have set back the best men I dispatched.' As he observed the man, the king pictured him leading his troops. He turned to the aide and said, 'Let him have six months instruction and send him south with a general's rank and pay.' Finally, as the king was ready to dismiss the case and leave, he asked the man:

'Do you accept this appointment?'

'No thank you, sire,' replied the man curtly.

The expression on the king's face remained unchanged. The king was disappointed but his royal status precluded he show any feelings. The man had impressed him well, and he was convinced this was the sort of man he needed down south. In the same tone he had used to appoint him general he communicated his sentence to the aide. He would be locked up in a dungeon until his bones rotted. A long silence filled the audience hall. Finally the people who had been absolved started to move on, guided by the guards.

From the moment he ordered him locked up the king could not take his mind off the man. The dungeon was minute. Orders were for no one to draw near, so food was pushed in through a narrow slot at the base of the massive iron gate, which remained always shut. For a short while in the afternoon, the sun would shine through the cell's single window. Since the cell gate was never opened, the man had pushed his cot across to take in the rays.

One day the king went down to see the man.

The routine of sounds to which the man had grown accustomed was altered. The sound of bolts unfastening, unmoved to that day, was a change in the routine of the food slot opening and closing. Following the king's orders, the guard gave the gate a push, but as the cot was wedged between the gate and the opposite wall, the gate would not open. The guard did not dare utter a word and, for want of something to occupy his time, gave the gate a new shove. Observing the guard's futile efforts, the king elbowed the guard out of the way and gave the gate himself a try, while he peeped through the slot, realizing it was the cot that obstructed his efforts.

"How dare you jam this gate?" raged the king. "Open up!"

His words were as imperative as usual, but his tone changed as he understood he was a different man.

"Open up," he insisted. "Let me out!"

If I have a problem with someone, it may turn out that this someone has nothing to do with the problem. It is evident that our outlook on the world bears an important effect on our behaviour, just as our behaviour affects our relationships. Some see a half-full glass, some see a half-empty glass... while others (according to Gary Larsson) yell, 'Hey! I ordered a hamburger!'

About the different ways to interpret a particular thing, the following story is a classic that fits in fine.

122. Christmas Presents

There were twin brothers who were the spitting image of each other but had opposite personalities. One was very optimistic while the other was hopelessly pessimistic.

It was Christmas Eve, and, as the twins went to bed, their parents laid out their presents by the fireplace, as if Santa Claus had left them there for them. The presents were two fantastic replicas of railway locomotives. It had been the intention of the parents that the twins discovered the presents the following morning. However, the twins' elder brother came home late that night and, seeing the twins' presents, he thought he would pull a little trick on them. He went back out in search of some fresh horse manure, which he collected in a bag. He then replaced the optimistic twin's locomotive with the contents of the bag, being careful to leave the nametag correctly placed. As soon as the twins were awake the next morning, they rushed downstairs to the fireplace, like they had done on so many Christmas days before. Their parents were still relaxing in bed when they heard the excited cries of the twins, and called them up.

'Come on up boys, tell us what Santa gave you.'

It was pessimistic Rupert who spoke first.

'I got an electric locomotive. It's imported... getting spare parts is going to be tough. The Japanese get rid of all their faulty stuff. They just ship it over, and we're the fools that accept everything. Besides, seeing how unstable our power supply has been at home lately, this thing's going to burn out in no time."

'What about you, Stanley, what did Santa bring you?'

'He brought me... a horse, a horse! It's not there now, but he'll be back!'

There are also those who will say a pessimist is nothing but a well-informed optimist, casting a mocking shadow of blissful ignorance over the optimistic spirit. Many will defend a pessimistic negative attitude and call it realistic. These people take it on as their duty to destroy the fantasy of others, who would otherwise embark upon adventures doomed to fail. In other words, a certain tension exists between the optimistic and the pessimistic for which there seems to be no solution.

However, there is a solution.

123. Looking After Sprouts

Two men were left in charge of surveillance at a remote national park. Canned food and supplies were flown in by helicopter. Before long, the men grew tired of canned food and one of them dug a small vegetable patch, with no previous experience. The other man, who knew all kinds of poisonous plants grew naturally in that part of the country, promptly destroyed the vegetable garden as soon as the first sprouts emerged.

He explained to his friend, 'It is impossible to tell the vegetables from the poisonous plants at first sight. The sprouts are very similar. I know it would have been hard for you to destroy your own work. You were full of enthusiasm, and the longer you worked at your project, the more you would have cherished it. Obviously there is little point in eating a lot of fresh vegetables if in doing so you consume a toxic plant and die of food poisoning. A balanced outlook from a realistic person was required, or your enthusiasm would have carried us to our grave.

The man who had started the vegetable garden was furious but had to admit his friend had a point, so they went on with their preserved food diet. After some time, their diet, lacking in fresh food took its toll, and their health noticeably deteriorated.

One day an old man stopped at their camp with his mule and stayed overnight with them. The arrival of a visitor called for a celebration and they uncorked a couple of bottles of wine. Their mood soon picked up with the wine and they told the old man the story of the vegetable garden. They were both keen on showing how wrong the other had been.

The old man told them neither of the two were wrong. 'It's just a question of opportunity,' he said. 'There is a time for planting. Do it enthusiastically and energetically; plant a lot of different seeds and don't worry about a thing."

The pessimist eyed the old man bitterly. 'When the sprouts start coming up you just let them grow,' the old man went on.

'Both of you'll need to water and care for the tiny plants as if all of them were good. When they reach a suitable size, you'll be able to tell by their shape which ones are poisonous and which are fit to eat. If you rush to kill the sprouts when they all look the same, you'll be sure not to eat poison, but you won't eat any vegetables either.'

When it was time to say good-bye, the pessimist walked the old man to his mule.

'Now, if you had to choose one of the two approaches, what makes more sense, to be a dreamer or to have one's feet on the ground?'

'The problem with having your feet on the ground is that you can't change your pants,' the old man chuckled as he left.

It is popular belief that both parties must yield their positions to conclude a successful negotiation. Those of us who preach win-win negotiation believe that when this happens both parties lose. Imaginative solutions are required. The old man's recommendation to the two men was that they use their skill and judgment to the maximum limit, but at different times; to be earnest and enterprising when it is time to plant and cultivate, and to be obsessively cautious once the plants have grown and it is time to tell the good ones from the bad ones.

It is a brainstorm approach. All assessment is put off in order to encourage creativity. Every idea is recorded, no matter how costly, unfeasible or hazardous it may appear to be. Solutions may be found to each of the objections to these ideas, but, if we crush an idea in its nest, we deny it the chance to develop and show whether it can be useful or not. Besides, if allowed to flow, one idea can lead to another, better idea.

We must remember that we are immersed in time, and time is mainly spent on implementation. As far as possible we should respect all opportunities to imagine and create, and avoid contaminating them with prejudice. Opportunity is a fundamental factor.

Here is another story that proves this.

124. No Styrofoam

Research conducted among car buyers has revealed certain patterns in their behaviour. Once their mind is made up about the model they are after, they shop around several dealers trying to seek out the best price, financing, and any freebies on offer. As a rule, they would gather a few facts at the first dealer, and then move on to a second dealer who offered roughly the same conditions except he was in a position to argue over points claimed by the first dealer in a convincing manner, since he had the last word. The third dealer held a similar advantage over the second dealer, and so on. Most buyers purchased their car at the last dealer they visited, either on the spot or on a future date on which they returned to close the deal on the basis of the information they had managed to gather.

One dealer who had access to the report on consumer behaviour rapidly adopted a promotional strategy to become the last in being consulted. Each buyer who walked in was offered a half-gallon of ice cream as a gift. It was the best quality ice cream in town, but it was packed in a non-thermal container. This meant the ice cream would melt in about ten minutes. People did not feel comfortable driving on to the next dealer while the ice cream melted in their car. So most of them went home to put the ice cream in their fridges, which often dispelled their price-hunting plans. When they were ready to close a deal, they returned to the dealer they had last visited. A memorable example of a process interrupted at the right time.

Throughout the process of negotiation, there are changes in humour. The climate of negotiation varies. A negotiator in command of the situation can focus her attention in order to perceive this. She behaves like a dancer on the floor. A very particular dancer who has the capacity to both dance and observe from the audience. Some discussions move in circles, and, when they seem to have moved away from the starting point, they go back and repeat the same arguments over their initial positions. More than likely, in these cases, there is a high rate of non-processed emotions. Parties need to go over and over the issues that trouble them. A negotiator who is in control of herself may perceive this, and avoid falling into the temptation of making any remark that will take the discussion back to square one. On the contrary, she will recognise the value of conceding a point and keep silent rather than lose precious ground.

125. Let Them Be, Woman

Gato Ortega's wife was reprimanding her daughter, a grown up woman who had several children of her own, because the children ran around barefoot all day.

'It's good for them,' the younger woman argued.

'They are stepping on dirty things in the cold. How can that be good? They are going to be ill!'

'Precisely, they don't catch cold because they are used to it. It makes them healthier and naturally stronger.'

'Why not have them run around naked and eat on the floor like pigs? That would be natural!'

A sister of the woman who argued in favour of going barefoot walked in and took sides in the argument, undoubtedly reminded of some earlier encroachment on her own rights.

'This is ridiculous, Mother,' she said. 'My sister has the right to raise her children anyway she pleases.'

'It is even more ridiculous to have them walk around looking like orphans,' the mother retorted. Then, feeling suddenly outnumbered, she tried to include Gato in the conversation.

'What do you think of these children that look like street boys?'

The daughters were unwilling to remain silent and give Gato an opportunity to back up their mother. They both talked simultaneously and heatedly defended their right to raise their children their own way, the freedom of the children's feet from stifling industrial footwear, contact with nature, and abolition of narrow-minded ideas on child raising.

When there was a moment of silence, Gato murmured to his wife in resignation, 'Let them be, Woman. Let them educate their way. Our way has turned out monsters.'

Those who have a clear idea of what they want are less attracted to arguments. During negotiations it is tempting to appear skilful, clever, and resourceful, impress the other party with sharp remarks, and brilliantly point out flaws in the other party's reasoning. No doubt our Ego will be grateful. But, is that what really counts? To take it a step further, the question is, are we clear on what the main issue is?

126. The Value of Miracles

In a wonderful small book called *Brief and Extraordinary Stories*, Borges tells about a yogi who came to the side of a river he needed to cross. As he lacked the three coins the ferry charged to take him across, he walked over the waters. Another yogi who heard about this feat said the miracle was not worth more than three coins.

How much are things worth? It is important to know this before starting a negotiation. How much things are worth to the other party and, hardest of all, what are they worth to me?

127. What is it Worth to Me?

A friend of mine went to interview a businessman at his home. The man had raised a sizeable fortune in different lines of business, mainly due to his skills as a merchant. He was a sullen and uncommunicative person and the distrusting look in his eyes made people who dealt with him come away with a feeling he must be annoyed with them, as if they owed him something. For some years now he had been living in a large, rather odd-looking flat, where he didn't seem to have finished moving his belongings to. The decoration was incomplete, and there were piles of unopened cardboard boxes in some corners. Through the large windows overlooking the river and the city the balcony lay strewn with empty flower pots. It was a high-storey building, no doubt worth a fortune. My friend and the man went about discussing their business and came to an agreement. As they were saying good-bye, out of politeness, my friend congratulated him on the superb flat.

"Do you really like it?" the man asked, showing more interest than the subject afforded.

"Yes," my friend was cornered into emphasizing an answer he hadn't actually considered.

"Well I don't," said the man.

"Why would you, who could choose to live anywhere you wanted, live in a flat you don't like?"

"It's just that, as I didn't like it from the start, I bargained it down to a price for which I couldn't possibly ever get a flat I like."

What was worth more to this man, a good bargain, a cheap buy, or an enjoyable place to live in?

At times we hear inward voices which want different things. When we choose to satisfy one voice, another voice complains. Those who suffer from this inward conflict don't make good team-mates for a creative relationship. One had better get on to some inward tidying up before starting a relationship, where one will encounter outside difficulties, against which one can only export confusion. Luckily there are genies that inhabit lamps, and they can offer useful teachings.

128. Wisdom and Wishes

A shepherd looking for a missing goat stumbled upon an old oil lamp, half buried in the sand. He thought he could use it to read at nights and took it home. Back home, he rubbed it with a cloth to clean it. The lamp puffed slightly and some kind of vapour flowed from its spout. The vapour gradually grew into a cloud that filled the room.

A pair of eyes materialized in the cloud and then a face that gazed at him with a gentle smile and said, 'Sir, I am the genie in this lamp and I will grant you any three wishes you ask for.'

When the man was able to recover from his amazement, he dared to ask shyly, 'What sort of things may one ask?'

'There is no limit, you may ask for anything you fancy.'

'Anything?' the man asked hesitantly.

'It will suffice that you can ask for it for me to be able to grant it.'

'Well then,' the man pondered. 'This is a decision one must make wisely.'

And after a moment's thought he continued: 'I shall use my first wish to ask for wisdom in making a correct choice of the other two wishes.'

'Granted,' the genie exclaimed, as a flurry of sparks circled around the man's head. 'What else will you ask for?'

The look on the man's face had changed. He stared at the genie out of his newly acquired wisdom and said, 'I ask that you cancel my remaining two wishes, thank you.'

An added advantage of having clear objectives is that they behave as a vaccine against reactive devaluation, a 'disease' that can make us devalue an idea for the sole reason it is being supported by the other party. My friend Ruben Steinberg sent me the following story, which spices up the issue with a touch of traditional Jewish culture.

129. A Day Ruined

One day a group of students saw a Jewish 'Kuentenik', a travelling merchant who basically sold clothes and linen articles. They approached the merchant and asked him what a pair of trousers cost. The man gave them a price which was overvalued, as he expected that, according to custom, they would enter a bargaining process that would end at a just price. However, the students were pleasantly surprised and showed it, as they found the price lower than anticipated. They paid and left. The merchant was disheartened. He bitterly regretted not having started off at a higher price. He closed his bags and went home. The day was already ruined.

In judo, the opponent's force is used for self-benefit. This concept is worth remembering during a negotiation with a slightly different approach. We wouldn't use the other party's strength against them. We would consider that their work can be useful to us, and give them a chance to get on with it. In other words, there are times when silence is our best tool, since it will allow the other party to think and develop their decision-making process. Letting the other party do their work is good advice.

A story that illustrates this point was related by a participant at one of my courses during a workshop debate.

130. Over Cheering

Some consultants on leadership and teamwork believe in taking their pupils for outdoor group activities, such as climbing mountains, log structures or ropes, similar to those used in training elite troops for combat.

Needless to say, security precautions are taken at dangerous climbing exercises, and participants wear protective harnesses which prevent them from crashing to the ground in the event of a fall. Anyway, at a considerable height, nobody is too keen on falling into thin air, and putting the harness to the test. All this turns this kind of exercise into a truly intense experience.

Our man in this story was part of a team which competed against others in a physical exercise. The exercise consisted of climbing to the top of a considerably high pole, and standing on a small platform, roughly the size of both feet together, which was fixed to the top of the pole. The hard part was to go from the climbing position to the standing position on such a small board. After leaning their hands and then their chest on the board, participants had to find a way to get their feet on it.

Then, as they looked down at the surrounding abyss, they would have to frantically push their stretched and exhausted muscles to raise their bodies steadily over the board. There was nothing to hold on to, and fear of falling had to be constantly fought back.

Participants had already gone through other exercises and were excited by the team spirit and their eagerness to compete. They cheered their team-mates fervently. Despite the enthusiastic (almost fanatical) cheering of the men and women who were part of our friend's team, no one in the team had managed to stand at the top without falling. Climbing was hard enough, but the manoeuvre required to get on one's feet at the top without losing one's balance was petrifying. By the time it was our friend's turn, the team had gradually lost hope in accomplishing the mission, but they cheered on as enthusiastically as ever.

Then our friend dared do something the others had not. He asked them to remain silent. The operation was delicate and needed to be approached with concentration. He knew what he had to do, and outside stimulation meant nothing but distraction.

With just the sound of the wind in his ears, his body shaking from the exertion and vertigo, he inched his body up through slight, cautious movements, until he was able to stand up and complete the mission. He had accomplished it with the help of his team-mates, who had been wise to leave him in peace at the crucial time.

As he watched his team-mates fail at previous attempts, he had wondered whether peer pressure did not have a negative effect in this case. He was able to draw a concept from his own experience, a concept he could generalize and incorporate to theory. Many people prefer to follow recipes. I believe it is more enriching to experiment and profit from the experience one has lived through.

How much can be learnt, and how much is already part of the talent one is born with?

How far should one follow theory and how far should one follow one's intuition?

How long need one keep researching before making a decision, and how much of the delay is due to lack of courage?

These are questions each one must answer.

I believe that knowing that at one point we will have to take a stand where our interest is at stake is good preparation and it sharpens our determination.

I appreciate the metaphorical value of a story referred to me by my Uruguayan colleague, Julio Decaro.

131. Where Does the Answer Lie?

Two young disciples had learned much from an old wise man. They had never heard him say something that was not true. His wisdom seemed unlimited. There came a time when they needed to come out of their shell and challenge him, in order to spread their own wings. They began questioning that he knew everything. Some of their class-mates regretted their attitude.

'Of course he knows everything,' said one of them. 'He knows through revelation, for he is one and all.'

'Ha!' replied one of the rebel youths. 'I suppose you believe he can tell the future.'

'Only one who has exceeded him in wisdom can talk about him in that way.'

Later one of the rebel youths told the other:

'I have a way of putting an end to this. See this tiny yellow bird? I shall hide it in my hand and take it before the Master, and I'll ask him whether it is dead or alive. If his answer is alive, then I'll open my hand for everyone to see the little bird fly away. If his answer is dead, I'll quickly squeeze it so that it's dead when I open my hand.

They went up to the Master when he was with all his disciples and posed the question in public. Everyone stared at the fisted hand the youth held forward.

The Master looked at his disciple in the eyes, smiled imperceptibly and then said, 'The answer lies in your hands.'

Roger Fisher's wife tells us that soon after her husband published *Getting to Yes* and before it became a bestseller translated into dozens of languages, she went into a bookstore and asked for directions, as she could not find the book. The sales clerk frowned and said dubiously, 'Look in the sex section.'

As first-time book writers we go through moments of anxiety that would con-tribute excellent ideas to a tragicomedy script. I know of one author who has bought copies of her own book several times over. Apparently she can't help going into bookshops and inquiring about her book pretending to be an ordinary customer. When she is actually shown a copy, she is usually too embarrassed to find an excuse that will let her out of the situation in a casual way. So she ends up paying for the book, and she walks out of the store trying to look like she is carrying something really valuable, wondering whom she can give the book as a present to this time.

On the subject of bookshops, I have a story of my own.

132. Bookshop Clerk

Shortly after my first book was published, I walked into a bookshop but could not find my book. It was not on display in the shop window, nor on the table at the entrance. I gave the clerk the name of the book and asked for help. She gave me the look of a person whose brain is scanning hundreds of book covers stored in her memory. The cloudy look in her eyes told me the search was not being successful. She started walking hesitantly and disappeared among rows of marginal bookshelves. After what seemed to me a very long time, the book materialized. The location was far from privileged. Where my book was displayed, no reader would accidentally stumble on it. My goal to spread the virtues of creative negotiation was not being well served this way. What could I say to her? I did not want to play the part of the un-objective parent who believes his children are special and deserve special privileges. But in order to comply with what I preached I needed to work on her interests. I couldn't imagine how to establish a conversation on interests just like that and out of the blue.

I let a while go by and said, 'If there were a story about you in one of these books, wouldn't you display the book in a more noticeable place?'

The question was unexpected and it took the clerk a few seconds to grasp the situation. I assumed it was unusual for a customer to ask this sort of question.

'If this book had a story about you, would you put it in a better location?' I asked thinking that if that did not make an impact on her interests, it would at least arouse her curiosity.

I didn't feel too comfortable doing what I was doing. I thought the clerk might feel offended, but I wanted to push on. It was time for action. I opened the book on this very page and turned it around for her to be able to read.

When she was finished reading the story, I told her I was very happy to have created a story whose ending had not yet taken place and was in her hands.

I don't know whether this business of trying to persuade bookshop clerks that this is a great book is lawful. I am convinced that ideas leading to win-win negotiation must be broadcast on a wider basis. I also think that these stories will help people who would normally never buy a book on negotiation theory come in contact with these ideas. I have no qualms in recommending these stories since most of them are not my own creation. As I first heard each one of them, I felt motivated to pass them on.

As in negotiations, there is a time for listening and understanding, and there is a time for assertiveness, defending what one believes in and pointing out its advantages.

On this subject, a story told to me by Patricio Nelson steals the show.

133. The Monkey

As a man had stopped to pick up his friend with whom he played tennis, he was surprised to see his friend say good-bye to a monkey and issue the monkey a few instructions before he left the house.

'I hope you don't mind my being curious,' said the man. 'Do you keep a monkey at home?'

'Yes, a trained monkey.'

'Doesn't someone need to stay with it?'

'No. Whatever for?'

'I was under the impression monkeys were awfully messy, and can be little buggers when they want to.'

'No, on the contrary. As I said, this is a trained monkey.'

'Does it behave well?'

'He's trained to do all kinds of housework. He washes dishes, cleans the house, and makes beds.'

'Are you serious?'

'Sure, this is a Zambian monkey. Down there there's a long-standing tradition on this.'

'Wow! I could certainly use something like that. I've only just separated and I was never any good with housework. I'm hopeless. I need help badly.'

'Look, I'm in the process of moving to England for a couple of years. I was thinking of selling him.'

'I could be interested, how much are you asking?'

'Three thousand dollars.'

'Oh my God!'

'Yes, they're not exactly cheap, but look at it this way, if he lives another ten years, he'll only cost you three hundred dollars a year. He mows the lawn, fetches your newspaper, receives and sends faxes, gives you a good back rub, and vacuums your swimming pool.'

'Really, you can't beat that. It sounds wonderful. Call it a deal.'

The man paid the three thousand dollars and went off with the monkey. Four days later he called his friend in a fury.

'Man, this monkey is a disaster! Forget cleaning the house and making beds, he chews up everything he finds. He doesn't understand a single instruction.'

'Listen Pal,' the friend unsuccessfully tried to slip a word in.

'He mucks up all over the place! He tears up curtains and upholstery, goes around smashing ornaments and glasses. This is a calamity! A public enemy!'

'Listen Pal,' insisted the friend. 'Speak well of the monkey... follow my advice... speak well of the monkey if you want to sell it.'

A German saying recommended, 'Don't go around saying you are an ass, or you'll run the risk someone will want to put a saddle on you.'

Although the monkey seller crosses the thin line of ethics, it's still a good story and one often finds an opportunity to tell it to someone who puts herself down too much.

Index

As detailed in the introduction, this is an index of suggested stories that bear relevance to the suggested headings. It is meant as a guide. The numbers are the story numbers, not the page numbers.